Sylvia Plath: A Very Short Introduction

VERY SHORT INTRODUCTIONS are for anyone wanting a stimulating and accessible way into a new subject. They are written by experts, and have been translated into more than 45 different languages.

The series began in 1995, and now covers a wide variety of topics in every discipline. The VSI library currently contains over 750 volumes—a Very Short Introduction to everything from Psychology and Philosophy of Science to American History and Relativity—and continues to grow in every subject area.

Very Short Introductions available now:

ABOLITIONISM Richard S. Newman
THE ABRAHAMIC RELIGIONS
    Charles L. Cohen
ACCOUNTING Christopher Nobes
ADDICTION Keith Humphreys
ADOLESCENCE Peter K. Smith
THEODOR W. ADORNO
    Andrew Bowie
ADVERTISING Winston Fletcher
AERIAL WARFARE Frank Ledwidge
AESTHETICS Bence Nanay
AFRICAN AMERICAN HISTORY
    Jonathan Scott Holloway
AFRICAN AMERICAN RELIGION
    Eddie S. Glaude Jr.
AFRICAN HISTORY John Parker and
    Richard Rathbone
AFRICAN POLITICS Ian Taylor
AFRICAN RELIGIONS Jacob K. Olupona
AGEING Nancy A. Pachana
AGNOSTICISM Robin Le Poidevin
AGRICULTURE Paul Brassley and
    Richard Soffe
ALEXANDER THE GREAT
    Hugh Bowden
ALGEBRA Peter M. Higgins
AMERICAN BUSINESS HISTORY
    Walter A. Friedman
AMERICAN CULTURAL HISTORY
    Eric Avila
AMERICAN FOREIGN RELATIONS
    Andrew Preston
AMERICAN HISTORY Paul S. Boyer

AMERICAN IMMIGRATION
    David A. Gerber
AMERICAN INTELLECTUAL
    HISTORY
    Jennifer Ratner-Rosenhagen
THE AMERICAN JUDICIAL SYSTEM
    Charles L. Zelden
AMERICAN LEGAL HISTORY
    G. Edward White
AMERICAN MILITARY HISTORY
    Joseph T. Glatthaar
AMERICAN NAVAL HISTORY
    Craig L. Symonds
AMERICAN POETRY David Caplan
AMERICAN POLITICAL HISTORY
    Donald Critchlow
AMERICAN POLITICAL PARTIES
    AND ELECTIONS L. Sandy Maisel
AMERICAN POLITICS
    Richard M. Valelly
THE AMERICAN PRESIDENCY
    Charles O. Jones
THE AMERICAN REVOLUTION
    Robert J. Allison
AMERICAN SLAVERY
    Heather Andrea Williams
THE AMERICAN SOUTH
    Charles Reagan Wilson
THE AMERICAN WEST Stephen Aron
AMERICAN WOMEN'S HISTORY
    Susan Ware
AMPHIBIANS T. S. Kemp
ANAESTHESIA Aidan O'Donnell

For more information visit our website

www.oup.com/vsi/

Heather Clark

SYLVIA PLATH

A Very Short Introduction

OXFORD
UNIVERSITY PRESS

Great Clarendon Street, Oxford, OX2 6DP,
United Kingdom

Oxford University Press is a department of the University of Oxford.
It furthers the University's objective of excellence in research, scholarship,
and education by publishing worldwide. Oxford is a registered trade mark of
Oxford University Press in the UK and in certain other countries

Published in the United States of America by Oxford University Press
198 Madison Avenue, New York, NY 10016, United States of America

British Library Cataloguing in Publication Data
Data available

Library of Congress Control Number: 2024940785

ISBN 978-0-19-884147-0

Printed and bound by
CPI Group (UK) Ltd, Croydon, CR0 4YY

Contents

Publisher's acknowledgements

We are grateful for permission to include the following copyright material in this book.

Excerpt(s) from *The Unabridged Journals of Sylvia Plath* by Sylvia Plath, edited by Karen V. Kukil, copyright © 2000 by the Estate of Sylvia Plath. Faber and Faber Ltd (world excluding US and Canada). Anchor Books, an imprint of the Knopf Doubleday Publishing Group, a division of Penguin Random House LLC (US and Canada). All rights reserved.

Excerpt(s) from *The Bell Jar* by Sylvia Plath. Copyright © 1971 by Harper & Row, Publishers, Inc. Used by permission of HarperCollins Publishers, and Faber and Faber Ltd.

Quotations from sixteen letters from The Letters of Sylvia Plath Volume 1 & 2 by Sylvia Plath. Copyright © 2017 by The Estate of Sylvia Plath. Used by permission of HarperCollins Publishers, and Faber and Faber Ltd.

Excerpts from The Collected Poems, Sylvia Plath. Copyright © 1960, 1965, 1971, 1981 by the Estate of Sylvia Plath. Editorial material copyright © 1981 by Ted Hughes. Used by permission of HarperCollins Publishers, and Faber and Faber Ltd.

List of illustrations

Chapter 1
Icon and iconoclast

Sylvia Plath is probably the best-known American woman poet of the 20th century. Her poems and fiction, especially her 1963 novel *The Bell Jar*, are widely taught in high schools and universities across the English-speaking world, while her *Journals* and *Letters* constitute one of the most important coming-of-age narratives of a woman writer in any era. Her name is regularly invoked in popular culture, often as shorthand for rebellion, feminism, or depression—and sometimes all three. Tragically, Plath is also well known for her death: she died by suicide when she was 30, shortly after the publication of *The Bell Jar*, and just a few months after she and her husband, the British poet Ted Hughes, separated. She left behind two small children and an oeuvre whose legal ownership passed to Hughes, who published some of Plath's most important work after she died.

During her lifetime, Plath (Figure 1) was well known in elite British and American literary circles as a talented poet, but she never saw the mass success she had always hoped for. The first and only poetry collection published in her lifetime, *The Colossus*, had a print run of only 500 copies and won no major prizes, though it received excellent reviews. Plath's novel *The Bell Jar* also received good reviews in the British press, but none were strong enough to propel the book onto the bestseller list. She had hoped the novel would earn enough money to finance her newly independent life as

1. Sylvia Plath in her Wellesley, Massachusetts backyard, 1954–55.

a single mother and writer, but in January of 1963, nothing indicated that *The Bell Jar* would go on to sell over three million copies; that her posthumously published poetry collection *Ariel* would become one of the most influential of the 20th century; or that Plath herself would become an international icon.

Indeed, Plath's contemporary iconic status as a feminist, confessional, "mad" poet probably would have surprised her. These familiar categories need to be questioned, and revised. They do not capture what Tracy Brain has called "the other Sylvia Plath." As Jacqueline Rose has pointed out, Plath's work transcends any monolithic category—as does Plath herself. Though Plath's poetry and prose hew closely to her own life, she is a master of irony and performance who plays deftly with concepts of biographical truth. Often, her work reflects political, rather than personal, concerns. She is a cerebral, surrealist writer whose work nods back to modernism and forwards to postmodernism, yet that work is often interpreted as straightforward autobiography—"confession"—in ways that gloss over or ignore its ambiguities. This book will explore some of the clichés attached to Sylvia Plath and her work, and offer a more nuanced introduction to her writing and her life, which are not mere reflections of each other. Rather, they exist in a complex dialogue that makes ethical, political, and intellectual demands upon Plath's readers.

Plath and feminism

Plath's work not only helped change the sound and sense of poetry in English, it buttressed one of the great political movements of the 20th century: second-wave feminism. Indeed, Plath's work—especially poems like "Daddy," "Lady Lazarus," "Fever 103°," "Purdah," "Ariel," "Three Women," and "The Applicant"—speaks powerfully to issues of gender, power, and rebellion. Plath came of age in a sexist era when women were legally discriminated against: meaningful educational and professional opportunities for women were scant, and they were at the mercy of a financial system that made it difficult to obtain loans and other forms of credit. In 1950s America, women were pressured to become wives, mothers, and homemakers; the ethos of Cold War "containment"—an American political strategy to stop the spread of Soviet communism—became an influential, culturally conservative ideology that sought to keep families nuclear and "contained" in suburban homes. Plath's 1955 Smith College Commencement speaker, the Democratic politician and presidential candidate Adlai Stevenson, told the bright young women graduates that they should embrace the "humble role of the housewife" and focus their energies on their husbands' goals. With can openers in one hand and a baby in the other, they were to create a peaceful, disciplined home. This was the best way, Stevenson suggested, to contribute to society. "Once they wrote poetry, now it's the laundry list," he said. Stevenson was a liberal, and his belittlement of women's professional ambitions suggests the larger cultural disregard in which these women's hopes and dreams were held.

Plath managed to break through the gendered barriers of her time by virtue of her talent and determination. She won a Fulbright Fellowship to Cambridge University, traveled through Europe, published widely, and embarked upon a creative marriage with a fellow poet, Ted Hughes. She put off having children until she had achieved at least some of her professional goals. After her marriage devolved, she wrote poems of fury that accused both her husband and her sexist culture of mistreating women. When Plath ended her famous 1962 poem "Daddy," "Daddy, daddy, you bastard, I'm through," her words signaled to a generation of women that she had triumphed over "the Father" and all that patriarchy stood for. After Plath's death, and in the wake of Betty Friedan's 1963 *The Feminine Mystique*, Plath's work—increasingly published in women's magazines such as *Ms.*, *Redbook*, *McCall's*, and *Cosmopolitan*—become a feminist rallying cry. Whether Plath intended for poems like "Daddy" and "Lady Lazarus" to become veritable anthems of the women's movement is beside the point. By the time these poems were published in *Ariel* in 1965, the personal had become the political. Plath's liberating, triumphant, and sometimes vengeful verse was ahead of its time. For feminists, Plath's heroines—and Plath herself—speak truth to power.

Plath may have been surprised to find herself a feminist icon. She was no stranger to women's achievement: her mother had a college degree and worked for a time as a professor at Boston University, while Plath herself was educated at two renowned women's colleges—Smith College and Newnham College, Cambridge—where she was nurtured by prominent female professors. She had read and admired the work of women writers like Virginia Woolf, Sara Teasdale, H. D., Edna St. Vincent Millay, and Edith Sitwell. Yet Plath does not fit neatly into the modern definition of a feminist. Ted Hughes always maintained that she was "'Laurentian,' not 'women's lib'"—that is, a disciple of D. H. Lawrence's philosophy of sexual liberation. He felt she was used as a pawn by feminists for causes she herself would not have supported.

Hughes had a point: Plath often remarked to others that she had no intention of becoming what she sourly called, in letters home, a "career woman." She was repulsed by the culture of spinsterhood amongst the dons at Newnham College, Cambridge, and vowed not to follow the same path. She could be cruel, in her letters and poems, to "barren," childless women or to those who'd had an abortion, and she was fiercely competitive with other women whose literary achievements mirrored hers. She put her husband's work before her own, both practically and intellectually, and, for most of the marriage, she assumed the bulk of housekeeping and childrearing without complaint. But these behaviors were not so unusual for a white, educated, middle-class American woman in the 1950s. The feminist poet Adrienne Rich had taken on a similar role during her marriage to the Harvard economist Alfred Conrad before she experienced a rebirth as a feminist activist and lesbian in the 1960s. Later, Rich would describe her years as a housewife and mother as years spent sleepwalking; the impact of second-wave feminism had awakened her.

Plath might have reached a similar point had she lived to see the changes wrought by the women's movement. Because for all her outward conservativism, Plath *was* an iconoclast; she refused to abide by the sexist mores of the 1950s and 1960s dictating that women must choose between a family and a literary career. She believed in equality of opportunity for women—a basic feminist principle—and was enraged by the sexual double standard of her day. Plath wanted it all—and for a time, she had it all—before the idea of having both a family and a career became a feminist catchphrase. Her poems are some of the first, and finest, in the English language to describe women's experience from a woman's perspective, especially motherhood, post-partum anxiety, miscarriage, and childbirth. Plath, ahead of her time, wrote about these ideas in the early 1960s in her verse drama "Three Women" and in poems like "Morning Song," "Candles," "Parliament Hill Fields," "Nick and the Candlestick," and others. These works provide a radical, subversive, and defiant counternarrative to the sentimental depictions of childbirth and motherhood prevalent in American culture then and now. Indeed, Anne Stevenson called Plath "the first great poet of childbirth in the language." But, as we will see, Plath's work was not solely limited to women's concerns or a feminist agenda.

Plath and confessionalism

Plath's representations of gender and power are just one part of what makes her work so groundbreaking and influential. She is also master of her craft, a true poet's poet. Plath had poetic ambitions from the time she was young, and published her first poem in the *Boston Herald* when she was only 8. She intuitively understood rhyme and meter as a child, and quickly mastered several formal poetic techniques. Many of her earliest poems concerned the seasons, especially spring. She often wrote about landscapes; most of these nature poems were sentimental in the style befitting a young girl in the 1930s and 1940s. But some were fierce and full of wind-blown trees, stormy seas, blazing sunsets, and cold, ice-blue skies—early forays into the imagery that would mark her mature work. She published regularly in her schools' literary magazines and newspapers, and sent out dozens of stories and poems to magazines during high school. She was finally published in *Seventeen* and the *Christian Science Monitor* before she began college. In the following years, she cracked *Harper's*, *The Atlantic*, and, in 1958, her "Annapurna," *The New Yorker*. Throughout this time, Plath maintained the habits of a professional writer: she kept meticulous track of her submissions, and when a rejection came in, she simply sent her piece out to the next publication on her list. She was a marvel of efficiency and productivity, and usually stoic about her rejections.

Plath's poetry is often labeled "confessional," partly because of her association with other famous poets of this so-called school, such as Robert Lowell and Anne Sexton. But the label misrepresents what she achieved and encourages a simplistic approach to her work. At Smith College, Plath had tempered the bracing voice of her juvenilia and become a diligent practitioner of the well-made, mannered poetry then in vogue. Her verses were exquisitely crafted in the style of poet heroes such as Wallace Stevens and W. H. Auden. She often consulted a rhyming dictionary and thesaurus as she wrote villanelles and other formally intricate poems.

Her aesthetic direction began to shift at Cambridge University in 1956 when she met Ted Hughes and his friends, a band of young, rebellious poets tired of the "genteel" verse of "The Movement" that then dominated literary journals, and eager to shake up British poetry. Plath, too, was starting to feel that her own poetry was too timid, too precious. She would rediscover her earlier, "other" voice at Cambridge, the voice behind those adolescent poems of waves breaking on rocks and skeletal outlines of winter trees. At Cambridge, she began to embrace a more direct, less decorous style—more Yeats than Stevens. Already, she wanted to break out of what she called, in a February 1959 journal entry, her "glass caul." Hughes also worked towards a bolder poetic style during his Cambridge years. Both poets made considerable headway on this mutual project during their marriage.

In 1959, when Plath and Hughes were living as freelance writers in Boston, Plath audited Robert Lowell's poetry writing seminar at Boston University. It was here that Plath became close to the poet Anne Sexton. In this class, often cited as the birthplace of confessional poetry, Plath began to loosen her meter and tackle riskier subjects in her poetry, such as mental illness and suicide, which she had always considered taboo. Lowell's *Life Studies* (1959) and Sexton's *To Bedlam and Part Way Back* (1960)—parts of which were workshopped in Lowell's seminar—were important influences on Plath. The autobiographical poems of *Life Studies* had themselves been influenced by the Beats, whose work Lowell had heard during a West Coast reading tour in March and April of 1957. After this tour, Lowell said, his earlier poems seemed to him "distant, symbol-ridden, and willfully difficult...like prehistoric monsters dragged down into the bog and death by their ponderous armor." But Plath and Hughes always purported to disdain what they both considered the let-it-all-hang-out style of Beat poetry. Plath's contempt is on full display in her 1958 journal entry about a poetry reading by George Abbe. Both she and Hughes came away disgusted; Plath called Abbe a "huckster" and mocked his suggestion that "anyone can write." When Abbe "fished up a mood poem in his unconscious & wrote it on the blackboard," she and Hughes, Plath wrote, "got sicker and sicker." Plath used Abbe as a foil to develop her understanding of an authentic, earned poetry that did not cut corners. She found Abbe's use of personal revelations particularly galling: his poems were "about his boyhood, sob....As if poetry were some kind of therapeutic public purge or excretion. Ted & I left, disgusted, to go home to our private & exacting demons who demand every conscious and deep-rooted discipline, and work, and rewriting & knowledge."

Plath would change her mind about the value of confession; after she took Lowell's class, she began using personal details in her work more frequently. She seemed to embrace the confessional label in a 1962 interview with Peter Orr in London, in which she discussed her admiration for Lowell and Sexton, and her enthusiasm for this new "taboo" aesthetic. But reading Plath's poems and novel as straightforward, autobiographical confession trivializes Plath's artistry, and assumes no separation between her life and art. The confessional label is dangerous, in particular, for women like Plath (and Sexton) who suffered from mental illness and died by suicide, because it ties their art to pathology and reduces their work to an impulsive cry from the heart. Elizabeth Gregory has observed that Plath's and Sexton's suicides may "have distracted readerly and critical attention from the poetry's

8

artfulness. The paradox is that in their examination of the 'real' as experienced by the gendered subject, Sexton and Plath lay themselves open to familiar judgements that reduce women to bodies.... So while confession may offer a way out of old orders, that way also risks becoming a route back in." The confessional label itself prompts us to read an artful, allusive, and deeply ironic poem like "Edge" as a suicide note rather than a devastating feminist poem about women, silence, and power. As Jacqueline Rose has written, "No writer more than Plath has been more clearly hystericized by the worst of a male literary tradition."

In Plath's poems, the personal is often overshadowed by the allegorical, the existential, and the surreal—what she called her "weirdnesses." Early successes like "The Disquieting Muses," "Electra on Azalea Path," "The Colossus," and "Poem for a Birthday" are autobiographical, but "confess" little. Later, more controversial poems such as "Daddy" and "Lady Lazarus" seem, in Yeats's memorable phrase, to "walk naked." They are near-perfect examples of what the critic Al Alvarez called "extremist" verse, but they might also be read as ironic performances. As Jo Gill has written, confessionalism "functions less as a mirror than as a prism which first splits and then projects fractured and elliptical images of its subject." Indeed, Plath's technique is not so much confessional as it is modernist; she hints obliquely at personal struggles and vulnerabilities through Classical or mythic scaffolds in the manner of her modernist heroes T. S. Eliot, W. B. Yeats, and James Joyce. Plath uses speakers like Lady Lazarus, the murderous Clytemnestra-figure of "Purdah," or the Medea-figure of "Edge" to *distance* herself from these poems. Embedded within Plath's late explosive poems, too, are the sonically rich rhythms of a poet steeped in New Criticism.

Plath herself discussed confessionalism at a 1961 dinner party in London with M. L. Rosenthal, the man who coined the term "confessional poetry" in his 1959 review of Lowell's *Life Studies*.

She told him that a confessional poem would fall flat unless it transcended the personal. Rosenthal remembered:

> She was terribly interested in Lowell but characteristically she didn't say anything about him personally. What she was interested in and what she talked about quite a lot was the question of putting yourself right into the poem. And the problem of aestheticizing it, of transcending the material, of getting beyond the personal. We agreed about that: it could be done, it had to be done, it wasn't worth it unless you get past the personal.

Rosenthal's memory dovetails with what Plath told Peter Orr in 1962: "Personal experience is very important, but certainly it shouldn't be shut-box and mirror-looking, narcissistic experience. I believe it should be relevant and relevant to the larger things, the bigger things such as Hiroshima and Dachau and so on."

When we read Plath's poems as straightforward autobiographical "confessions," we miss an opportunity to engage with her ironic self-awareness, her literary sophistication, and her bookishness. As Plath wrote to her friend Phil McCurdy in 1954, "My bookcases are overflowing—shelves of novels, poetry, plays, with lots of philosophy, sociology & psych. I am a bibliomaniac." Plath, one of the most brilliant students of her generation, was able to draw upon her vast knowledge of Western literature as she composed her own work. Like the modernists before her, Plath's traditional poetic training allowed her to break from a tradition that had, for her, run dry and, as Ezra Pound exhorted his contemporaries, make it new.

Plath and "madness"

Sylvia Plath has become an icon of the "mad" poet, but the drama and tragedy of her death distract us from the power of her art. Male writers who died by suicide, such as Ernest Hemingway, Hart Crane, and David Foster Wallace, are not defined by their death as emphatically, or as negatively, as Sylvia Plath. Hermione Lee,

Virginia Woolf's biographer, has made the point that "Women writers whose lives involved abuse, mental illness, self-harm, suicide, have often been treated, biographically, as victims or psychological case histories first and as professional writer second." These words are especially true for Plath, who has often been pathologized in biographies, television, movies, and magazines. Plath's suicide provides her critics with an excuse not to take her art seriously—to equate her fame with her death—and, as the critic Janet Badia points out, to label her readers a "cult." Early reviews set the tone for such reductive characterizations: after *Ariel* was published in 1965, *Time* magazine called it "a jet of flame from a literary dragon who in the last months of her life breathed a burning river of bale across the literary landscape." The *Washington Post* called Plath herself a "snake lady of misery" in an article entitled "The Cult of Plath." Robert Lowell wrote an introduction to *Ariel* in which he connected Plath's suicidal tendencies to her poems—seeming to echo Alvarez's understanding of her as an "extremist" poet—while Ted Hughes also wrote reductively about Plath's dangerous muse in the years after her death. These men suggested that creating art had pushed Plath over the edge, when in fact the cause of her death by suicide was a mental health condition: depression. The act of writing was, for Plath, life-affirming—as necessary to her as breathing, as she told Orr in 1962. Plath's depression seemed to worsen during the periods when she felt incapable of writing.

If Hughes, Alvarez, and Lowell have linked Plath's "madness" to her creative drive, feminist literary criticism has frequently portrayed Plath's "mad" status as positive: that is, the madwoman as feminist rebel. Framed thus, Plath's mental illness is something to romanticize, and a powerful protest against the injustice she experienced in her sexist era. Indeed, Plath herself may have understood her artistic representations of madness in this way, especially in *The Bell Jar*. But there has been a movement within feminist disability studies to question this "madwoman-as-feminist-rebellion metaphor," as the critic

11

Elizabeth Donaldson calls it, popularized by Gilbert and Gubar's seminal work of feminist criticism, *The Madwoman in the Attic*. Madwoman theory seeks to critically examine this historical trope within literature and culture, to better understand its roots, and to push back against the idea that madness is a way for women to rebel against the patriarchal structures of their society. Disability scholars point out that mental illness is real, encoded within the body, and results not in power for women but powerlessness. Romantic glamorizations of Plath's "madness" and suicide as protest—or even performance—do Plath and other women afflicted with severe depression a disservice.

Biographers have been particularly guilty of pathologizing Plath and her desire to write, and have done harm to her legacy; reducing Plath to a "mad" poet diminishes her intellectual and creative achievement. What Elizabeth Hardwick once wrote of Lowell is also true of Plath: "He was not crazy all the time—most of the time he was wonderful. The breakdowns were not the whole story." Misrepresentations of Plath's mental illness began with her first biographer, Edward Butscher, who titled his book *Method and Madness* and, with no medical evidence, suggested that Plath was "schizophrenic." She was not. She suffered from depressions that struck periodically and with varying severity. (There seems to have been a strong genetic component; Plath's paternal grandmother died in a mental hospital, and Plath's son died by suicide.) Plath did not hallucinate, lose track of time, or hear voices. But she suffered at the hands of an unenlightened and sexist mental health industry in the early 1950s. Her first bout of depression, in the summer of 1953, was treated with electroshock therapy at a Boston-area asylum, Valley Head. The traumatic treatment, which was misadministered (and which she drew upon in *The Bell Jar*), left Plath in even deeper despair. When her depression worsened that summer, she felt, as she explained in a letter to a friend, that suicide was a better alternative to a future of electroshock therapy at the hands of paternalistic doctors in the bowels of an insane asylum. The more we learn about Plath's psychiatric treatment in the summer of 1953, the harder it is to untangle the motives for her suicide attempt from the trauma of her electroshock treatments at Valley Head. In 1963, when she was living in London and again suffering from depression, she was prescribed several different drugs whose interactions were not then well understood. These interactions could have made her depression worse. Plath's suicide attempt in 1953 and suicide in 1963 may have been partially triggered by her fear of the asylum and a life of institutionalization, in addition to her very real terror of losing her mind and her autonomy. Indeed, she wrote her psychiatrist a week before her suicide about her fear of "a mental hospital, lobotomies."

Plath herself made depression a theme of *The Bell Jar* and several of her greatest poems, including "The Moon and the Yew Tree," "Elm," "Sheep in Fog," and "Edge." Her ability to resurface from the depths and translate her harrowing experience into art makes her poetic portraits of depression amongst the most powerful in the English language. She is also one of literature's most compelling chroniclers of mental illness, and a critic of the mental health practices of her era. Her story "Johnny Panic and the Bible of Dreams" portrays electroshock therapy as terrifying, while *The Bell Jar*, originally marketed as a sensationalist college girl suicide story, is one of the great protest novels of the 20th century. There, Plath wrote scathingly about the psychiatric practices to which she was subjected in the 1950s, from condescending therapy sessions to botched electroshock therapy. "Madness" was a condition Plath explored as well as endured.

Plath and politics

When we read Plath as merely a confessional or "mad" poet, without further considering her irony, her allusions, her mastery of poetic forms, and her literary sophistication, we not only trivialize her artistry, we trivialize her political awareness and involvement. The idea that Plath was not a politically engaged person was too long taken for granted, even by influential feminist critics such as Sandra Gilbert and Susan Gubar, who wrote that Plath "did not have an explicitly political imagination." Elizabeth Hardwick, too, argued that Plath had "nothing of the social revolutionary in her." Joyce Carol Oates similarly claimed that Plath "exhibits only the most remote (and rhetorical) sympathy with other people" and that she only wanted to "define herself, her sorrows." This "selfishness" became a lens with which to view Plath in the 1970s, 1980s, and even 1990s. Such admonishments are tied to Plath's status as a confessional poet because they do not assume a split between the art and the artist. This mischaracterization allowed some critics to effectively dismiss Plath as uninterested in the crises of her day—she is, instead, a narcissistic navel gazer interested only in herself and her own crises.

These mischaracterizations have harmed Plath's legacy. Robin Peel's *Writing Back: Sylvia Plath and Cold War Politics* and Tracy Brain's *The Other Sylvia Plath* have shown that Plath did engage with the politics of her day. She was raised in a family that taught pacifism, an ideology she embraced all her life. Although her mother was a Republican, Plath herself was a Democrat who was disgusted by hawkish Cold War rhetoric and McCarthyism. Her middle school and high school papers, along with letters to her German pen-pal, reveal her disdain for war and the bomb; in high school she co-authored an article, "Youth's Plea for World Peace," published in the *Christian Science Monitor*, that disavowed hate and jingoistic nationalism, and preached pacifism. Plath's public embrace of pacifism was courageous, for in the early 1950s pacifism was a suspect ideology that could earn one a place on an FBI blacklist.

At Smith College, Plath wrote letters and diary entries about her disdain for the "Red Hunt," and booed Senator Joseph McCarthy when he came to speak on campus. She embedded these political stances in *The Bell Jar*, which she wrote in 1961 but which looked back to her breakdown, suicide attempt, and institutionalization in 1953. Plath begins her novel with a sentence about the looming electrocution of the Rosenbergs, who were sentenced to death for passing atomic secrets to the Soviets. As Elaine Showalter has noted, Plath's protagonist, Esther Greenwood, will also suffer a kind of electrocution, in the form of electroshock therapy, for her own "dissidence." Plath weaves these two stories together and connects Esther's "madness" to the sickness of her warmongering, sexist, racist, and homophobic society. The novel is a criticism of the Eisenhower era's repressions and their particularly stultifying effect upon women as much as it is the chronicle of a breakdown. Plath was steeped in the work of the philosopher Eric Fromm, whose book *The Sane Society* interrogated and reframed concepts of sanity and insanity as a response to culture. While we cannot be sure Plath read this book, she had read other work by Fromm as well as R. D. Laing's anti-psychiatry book *The Divided Self.* Ideas from these books hover over the pages of *The Bell Jar*: to what extent is Esther's sickness a result of living in a repressive, sexist, and unjust society?

Plath was committed to the anti-bomb movement and attended the CND march in London in 1960. She wrote to others in the early 1960s about her anxieties regarding nuclear fallout and her disgust for the American military industrial complex; many of her poetic speakers express a horror of nuclear war. Some of Plath's best-known poems, such as "Ariel" and "Lady Lazarus," were written during the tense days of the Cuban Missile Crisis in October 1962, and reflect this anxiety and unrest. Her close friend Elizabeth Compton Sigmund, who eventually became an environmental activist, remembered Plath's passionate interest in politics. After their first conversation in Devon, Plath told Sigmund how excited she was to have found what she called a "committed" woman. Sigmund thought Plath, had she lived, would have joined her on marches and environmental political campaigns. Sigmund's feeling echoes those of Plath's close friend from childhood and adolescence, Perry Norton (co-author of "Youth's Plea for World Peace"), who recalled her strong commitment to liberalism and pacifism. Indeed, Plath's contempt for Eisenhower's politics is clear in an extraordinary, ironic collage she made in 1960. In it, a smiling Eisenhower holds a deck of cards (Plath has affixed the word "sleep" onto his lapel), while to his right a war plane is poised to impale a woman in a swimsuit above the caption, "Every Man Wants His Woman on a Pedestal" (Figure 2).

2. Sylvia Plath's 1960 collage of the Eisenhower era.

Plath's use of Holocaust imagery in some of her poems has invited controversy. As we will see in Chapter 6, she has been criticized for what some critics see as an unethical appropriation of Jewishness. Recent evidence suggests Plath identified as part-Jewish (Plath's mother believed that her maternal Viennese grandmother was Jewish or part-Jewish) and may have felt bound to bear witness to the genocide. Plath also expressed guilt about the Holocaust to friends because her father was German and her mother Austrian-American. And she was publishing at a time when there was pressure for poets to write about the horrors of the Second World War. The influential critic Al Alvarez encouraged—goaded, even—English poets to write more honestly about these events in his landmark 1962 anthology *The New Poetry*. Plath was close to Alvarez, who was Jewish and had visited Auschwitz; they discussed the concentration camps together in the fall of 1962. Plath likely felt she was facing horrors other poets would not when she incorporated Holocaust motifs into her poems.

And yet, Plath was not above using racist or anti-Semitic language in her letters and work despite the fact that some of her closest friends and lovers were Jewish and African-American. Scholars have also called attention to Plath's ableism, especially regarding physical disability, which reflected the phobias, condescension, and prejudices of white, middle-class, mid-century American society. Still, much of Plath's work cries out against injustice experienced by women and the mentally ill. While it is true that Plath was not running political committees, she was not apolitical. She was busy raising two young children, managing a household, and acting as her husband's agent and secretary. She spent nearly all of her precious free time writing. As Linda Wagner-Martin has written, "To have written both *The Bell Jar* and her later poems surely speaks of a kind of outright defiance of societal norms." In the face of immense societal pressure to make herself small, to sacrifice her literary ambitions to her children and husband, writing was itself a political act.

Chapter 2
Origins and ambitions

"A fine, white flying myth"

Sylvia Plath was born in Boston, Massachusetts, on October 27, 1932, in the early days of the Great Depression. Her father, Professor Otto Plath, met Aurelia Schober, Plath's mother, when Aurelia was a student in one of his German language classes at Boston University. The young family lived first in Jamaica Plain and then moved to Winthrop, a seaside community north of Boston. Both of Plath's parents were of German heritage: Otto immigrated to America from the Polish Corridor when he was 15, and spoke German and Polish (his English retained a trace of a German accent); Aurelia was born in Boston, where her parents had emigrated from Austria. Plath's parents and grandparents all spoke German fluently, but Plath would struggle throughout her life to learn German.

Plath's parents were intensely literary and academic. Otto had a deep interest in German literature, and had written his Master's thesis at the University of Washington on Washington Irving's influence on the German Romantic author Wilhelm Hauff. Aurelia graduated valedictorian of her Boston University college class in 1928 and went on to complete her Master's degree in German and English there. By then, Otto had changed subjects in the wake of rising anti-German sentiment during the First World War and become a renowned entomologist with a doctorate from Harvard. Despite the 21-year age difference between them, the two married in January 1932. The marriage was not a happy one; Otto's earlier promises of a progressive partnership gave way to a more rigid, Teutonic, and traditional arrangement. Aurelia relinquished her dreams of holding salons with other university families: Otto did not enjoy socializing, and commandeered the dining room table with his books and papers.

Aurelia had her own literary ambitions, but, as a wife and mother during the Depression, she had no outlet for realizing them beyond assisting Otto with his scientific writings. She poured her ambitions into her children (Plath's brother Warren was born in 1935), amassing a large library of children's books and reading to them constantly. She often recited the poetry of John Donne, Robert Browning, W. B. Yeats, Alfred, Lord Tennyson, Samuel Coleridge, Emily Dickinson, T. S. Eliot, and others. Plath, a precocious child, recalled that her first literary frisson occurred when her mother read her Matthew Arnold's poem "The Forsaken Merman." Plath wrote of her pleasure at hearing the sibilant lines:

> Sand-strewn caverns, cool and deep,
> Where the winds are all asleep;
> Where the spent lights quiver and gleam;
> Where the salt weed sways in the stream...

In her 1962 memoir "Ocean 1212-W," Plath wrote that she felt "gooseflesh" on her skin when she first heard this poem. "Had a ghost passed over? No, it was poetry. A spark flew off Arnold and shook me, like a chill. I wanted to cry; I felt very odd. I had fallen into a new way of being happy." The poem's sea imagery also captivated her imagination, for Winthrop was a coastal town, and Plath spent hours swimming and playing on the beach as a

3. Sylvia Plath on Cape Cod, 1954.

child. In "Ocean 1212-W," she wrote with nostalgia of time spent fishing with her uncle Frank, long shore walks with her grandfather, and her grandmother's seafood stew. The memoir makes clear how intimately tied her life in Winthrop was to the ocean: "I sometimes think my vision of the sea is the clearest thing I own" (Figure 3). She also wrote of her intense relationship with the sea in her 1940s scrapbook.

Plath's other great love was poetry. She learned to read basic words when she was 3 years old, and by age 5 she could write. In December of 1937 she wrote her first two-lined poem, "Thoughts," about the joys of Christmas. Indeed, Plath had literary ambition from a very young age. Some of her earliest poems, written in 1940, survive in an illustrated book she made by hand. They show that by the age of 8 or 9 she understood how to use rhyme and meter; she wrote limericks, quatrains with a-b-c-b rhyme schemes, stanzas with regular iambic and dactylic meter, and even revised her work. Her very early poem "Snow" suggests her skill with meter and imagery:

> Snow, Snow sifting down
> Sifting quietly 'round the town
> Sending it a blanket of cold white
> To keep it warm every night.

In a playful twist, the snow makes the town warm. This was sophisticated use of paradox and irony for a child.

In 1940, Otto Plath died of complications resulting from undiagnosed diabetes. He had refused to see a doctor about his increasingly severe illness, and by the time one was summoned, it was too late. Plath was just 8 years old. She had been her father's favorite, and his death changed her life. Aurelia sold the Winthrop house and moved her family to the leafy, affluent suburb of Wellesley, just west of Boston. Wellesley had fine public schools, and, it was thought, a more favorable climate for Plath's younger brother Warren, who suffered from recurring bronchial illnesses. Otto had died with no pension and just enough life insurance to cover medical bills and the funeral. To cut expenses, Plath's maternal grandparents sold their own home in Winthrop and moved into the Wellesley house. The white clapboard colonial at 26 Elmwood Road was respectable but modest, and Plath had to share a room with her mother until she was in high school. Plath's grandfather worked as a maître d' at the nearby Brookline Country Club, where he boarded during the week. Plath's grandmother took charge of the children while Aurelia worked full-time teaching secretarial skills at Boston University. For Plath, the move to Wellesley marked the end of her childhood: she later looked back on her years in Winthrop as a "fine, white flying myth." Memories of Otto would inspire some of Plath's strongest poems, including "Electra on Azalea Path," "Full Fathom Five," "The Colossus," and "Daddy."

Early successes

The Wellesley household was a happier one, even though Plath missed her father deeply. She grew closer to her maternal Schober grandparents and flourished in Wellesley's top-rated public schools. She spent her afterschool hours in Girl Scouts or in the company of her many girlfriends, and attended Girl Scout sleep-away camps in Massachusetts and New Hampshire during her summers. But the war years were a tense time for the small German-Austrian family. Plath later wrote two short stories about this period, "Superman and Paula Brown's New Snowsuit" (1955) and "The Shadow" (1959). In both semi-autobiographical stories, a girl growing up in greater Boston during the war is bullied by neighborhood children on account of her Germanic heritage. In "The Shadow," the young narrator is haunted by a sense of anxiety, despite her faith in "parents, the police, the F. B. I., the President, the American Armed Forces." She finally realizes that her unease is due to her father's German background. Soon he is sent to a detention camp. Plath was 12 when the bomb was dropped on Hiroshima in 1945 and *Life* magazine published a story of Nazi atrocities. The horrors she learned about in her adolescence led her to embrace her parents' pacifism and her mother's Unitarianism. (Later, she would call herself an atheist.) The imagery of the Second World War and, eventually, the Cold War would feature prominently in her fiction and poetry.

Most of Plath's adolescent poems were sentimental landscape descriptions; spring and rebirth, themes that would animate many of her mature poems, were already leitmotifs. Other poems from the mid-1940s show Plath's growing command of complex metrical arrangements. In 1944's "Halloween," she alternates between perfect iambic tetrameter and trimeter. "A Winter Sunset," written when she was 13, possesses a spare grandeur and familiar imagery (moon, trees, frost, shifting light) that foreshadows the language of her later poems:

> The moon hangs, a globe of iridescent light
> In a frosty winter sky,
> While against the western glow one sees
> The bare, black skeleton of the trees.

Plath discovered Sara Teasdale as an adolescent, and copied several of Teasdale's poems, including "Late October" and "Beautiful, Proud Sea," into her diary. Plath continued publishing in various local and school papers, and winning many literary and art contests. Her ambition to become a great writer grew throughout her time in junior high school, when she spent long afternoons up in her yard's apple tree, reading and composing poems. She began a novel, titled *Stardust*, when she was 11 or 12, in which fairies reveal their magic to the heroine, a girl named Nancy. (The book comprised nine chapters by 1946 and 26 typed pages.) In 1947 Plath wrote a remarkable poem about her literary ambition, "Fireside Reveries," in which she declared, "My thoughts to shining fame aspire | For there is much to do and dare." Such ambition in a teenage girl was, at that time, considered immodest and unfeminine. But Plath always knew writing was her vocation.

At Wellesley's high school, Plath took a three-year honors seminar with a legendary English teacher, Wilbury Crockett, where she read the classics of American, English, and Russian literature. Plath served her first literary apprenticeship in Crockett's class. He later said Plath was the best student he had ever taught, and told Aurelia, during a parent–teacher conference, that Plath would be able to make writing "her career." It was in Crockett's class that Plath first grappled with formative texts such as Virginia Woolf's *Mrs. Dalloway* and T. S. Eliot's *The Waste Land*. She wrote many poems and short stories, which she sent out to magazines for publication. After over 50 rejections, Plath finally published a short story in *Seventeen* the summer after her senior year of high school, "And Summer Will Not Come Again." The story is sentimental and does not reflect the preoccupations or the style of several of her other high school stories, which focused on disappointed, lonely, or poor women on the margins of society. These stories are early iterations, perhaps, of Esther Greenwood's outsider's perspective in *The Bell Jar*. Plath's high school stories and poems were deeply influenced by the modernist poetry and fiction she was reading in Crockett's class, especially that of Yeats, Joyce, and Eliot. Several of her high school poems, such as "A Winter Sunset" and "Portrait" ("white flashes of cold | Lance my wings") display themes and images that mark her later poetry.

The Plath–Schober family was not wealthy; the two-generation household was cramped, and Plath took on odd jobs like babysitting, housecleaning, and dusting school offices. Still, Aurelia worked hard to fill her children's lives with music and art lessons, summer camps, and a seemingly limitless supply of books. A close friend from this time remembered, "Her mother had to scrape, and Sylvia knew that." Plath knew she would need a scholarship to fund an education at a top women's college. She applied herself rigorously to her academic and creative work, and, in 1950, was overjoyed to receive a nearly full scholarship to Smith College, a renowned all-women's college in western Massachusetts and one of the elite "Seven Sisters." The scholarship was generously funded in part by the writer Olive Higgins Prouty, who would play an important moral, financial, and pastoral role in Plath's life. Still, Plath envied her affluent peers who spent their summers in Europe while she strained her back picking strawberries at a local farm.

In the summer of 1950, Plath received her first fan letter from a young Jewish beatnik named Eddie Cohen. The two began an important correspondence that would last for several years. Eddie, who attended Roosevelt College in Chicago, was one of the few people to whom Plath could speak frankly about sex and politics. His freethinking leftist attitude influenced her own burgeoning philosophical positions on those subjects. As mentioned, Plath herself was a Unitarian who leaned atheist and, like her parents, a pacifist. (She read both Nietzsche and Emerson during this time, and preferred Nietzsche.) She did not support the Korean War, which she said made her "ill," and she called the decision to bomb Hiroshima a "sin." She even wrote anti-war poems for Mr. Crockett titled "Seek No More the Young," modeled on the war poetry of Wilfred Owen and Siegfried Sassoon, and "Youth's Appeal for Peace," which described "The tortured screams of a million men." In her 1950 article, "Youth's Plea for World Peace," co-authored with her friend and classmate Perry Norton and published in the *Christian Science Monitor*, the two took a pacifist position, rejecting the logic of the Cold War arms race and arguing for the "basic brotherhood of all human beings." They called nationalism a "dilemma." These were radical positions to adopt publicly during the communist witch-hunts of the McCarthy era. In 1951, she wrote her most political poem yet, "I Am an American," which mocked her nation's materialist, consumer culture. Americans were "baptized with Chanel Number Five | In the name of the Bendix, the Buick, and the Batting Average." She also called attention to American hypocrisy and xenophobia: "We all know that certain truths are self-evident: | That we believe in liberty and justice for all | Like the great green lady with the bronze torch | Lifted beside the door marked 'Members Only.'" Plath would become an increasingly passionate Democrat who was crushed when Dwight D. Eisenhower defeated Adlai Stevenson in the 1952 presidential election.

College poet

Plath entered Smith College in the autumn of 1950. There, she majored in English and took courses from famous professors such as Elizabeth Drew, Mary Ellen Chase, Alfred Kazin, and Robert Gorham Davis. Plath, a star student, received much support and encouragement from these faculty members. While she read women writers such as Virginia Woolf, Elizabeth Bowen, and Edith Sitwell, her education was grounded in male modernism: James Joyce, W. B. Yeats, T. S. Eliot, D. H. Lawrence, Wallace Stevens, and Dylan Thomas. These writers, especially Woolf, Yeats, Joyce, and Lawrence, became her literary touchstones.

Plath made several close friends at Smith, but she always felt—partly on account of her social class—that she would never embody the perfect Smith girl. Indeed, Plath received mixed messages at Smith in the age before second-wave feminism. Academic achievement was lauded and encouraged, but the goal of most Smith graduates in the early 1950s, it seemed, was to marry and have children. Adlai Stevenson codified this unspoken dictum when he told Plath's graduating class in 1955 that they should become mothers and housewives, and focus their energies on their husbands' goals. A popular tune at Smith made light of the dilemma:

> You're sharp as a pen point
> Your marks are really 10-point,
> You are Dean's List, Sophia Smith,
> But a man wants a kiss, kid,
> He doesn't want a Quiz Kid,
> Oh, you can't get a man with your brains.

Plath was a prolific college writer: she wrote scores of newspaper articles for the *Daily Hampshire Gazette* and the *Springfield Daily News* and continued to publish creative work in the *Smith Review*, the *Smith Alumnae Quarterly*, *Seventeen*, the *Christian Science Monitor*, and elsewhere. She threw herself into her studies and regularly received top grades, even in the science course she dreaded. Plath had already established a reputation as a college poet when in 1952 she won the prestigious *Mademoiselle* fiction contest with her short story "Sunday at the Mintons," about a lonely spinster who lives with her imperious brother. The brother in the story was based on Plath's boyfriend at the time, Dick Norton, the brother of her friend Perry Norton. They were unofficially engaged, but Plath was increasingly uncertain about marrying him. When Dick contracted tuberculosis at Harvard Medical School in 1952—necessitating a long stay in an upstate New York sanatorium—Plath grew apart from him and began dating other men. The two eventually broke up for good in 1953. Plath would base the character of Buddy Willard, in *The Bell Jar*, on Dick.

Plath published other short stories in *Seventeen* while at Smith—"Den of Lions," "Initiation," and "The Perfect Setup"—but perhaps her strongest story from the Smith years, "Mary Ventura and the Ninth Kingdom," remained unpublished until 2019. Plath wrote this surrealist allegory in December 1952 for a writing class. She had endured her first major depression that fall, and had considered suicide both in her journal and in a harrowing letter to her mother. "Mary Ventura" follows a female protagonist, Mary, on a Dantean train ride to an unknown destination, "the ninth kingdom." Mary learns from a grandmotherly passenger that this is "the kingdom of negation, of the frozen will." The reader begins to understand that Mary is hurtling towards suicide. After seeing another passenger forced off the train, Mary changes her mind, no longer frozen by depression, and asserts her will to live. She jumps off the train at the seventh kingdom, where it is spring, and a kindly older woman selling daffodils and roses welcomes her. Though the story is coded, it marked the first time Plath had written creatively about her own experience of depression and suicidal despair. "Mary Ventura" opened up a new vein in fiction for Plath that laid the foundation for later works such as "Tongues of Stone," "Johnny Panic and the Bible of Dreams," and *The Bell Jar*. In "Mary Ventura" Plath drew upon elements of autobiography, myth, classical literature, and surrealist imagery, just as she would in her *Ariel* poems. She had come a long way since the teen romance of "And Summer Will Not Come Again," but "Mary Ventura" was too surreal and oblique for the women's magazine market. *Mademoiselle* rejected the story in March 1953.

Plath's Smith-era poems display a preoccupation with form and sound, sometimes at the expense of meaning. She frequently consulted her dog-eared thesaurus for word choices. Her benefactress Olive Prouty thought that these poems bore a resemblance to "abstract paintings"—full of vivid colors, but obscure. Plath herself later called them "desperately Audenesque." Indeed, Auden was one of her poetic heroes and, in the spring of

1953, a visiting lecturer at Smith. Plath showed him some of her poetry, but his response was not as encouraging as she had hoped. Still, she was thrilled when her poems "Doomsday," "To Eva Descending the Stair," and "Go Get the Goodly Squab" were accepted by *Harper's* that spring—her first "Professional Acceptance," as she put it. "Mad Girl's Love Song," when it was published in 1953, also gained Plath fans—including the future Harvard poetry critic Helen Vendler, who wrote to Plath's mother calling the poem "the only decent villanelle in the English language besides Dylan Thomas's 'Do Not Go Gentle Into That Good Night'." Other poems from Plath's Smith years, such as "Morning in the Hospital Solarium," "Epitaph in Three Parts," and "Lament" (an elegy for her father), foreshadow later poems that deal with grief and loss, such as "Sheep in Fog" and "Words." "Circus in Three Rings" features a young woman who tames lions and walks a tightrope, and is an early iteration of ironic poems about gendered performances like "Aerialist" and "Lady Lazarus." If some of these poems now read like apprentice pieces, Plath's mastery of formal techniques, such as the villanelle, served her well later. She would embrace free verse and looser lines after she married Ted Hughes, but she never abandoned form entirely. Even in a poem like "Daddy," with its centrifugal velocity, Plath writes in regular, patterned stanzas. Her *Ariel* poems seem about to fly off the page, but Plath's careful and precise poetic structures act as guardrails. She always maintains a sense of authority and control.

Chapter 3
Cold War maladies

Breakdown

Near the end of her junior year at Smith in 1953, Plath won a prestigious summer internship at *Mademoiselle* magazine in Manhattan. She was assigned the role of Guest Managing Editor, and worked for a legendary boss, Cyrilly Abels. But Plath's experience in New York that summer left her feeling disoriented; Abels pushed her hard, and she was exhausted by continuous social events that revolved around the fashion and beauty industries. Plath also had a disastrous date with a Peruvian United Nations translator which, she hinted in her journal, involved sexual assault. By the end of her internship in late June 1953, she was reeling and close to breakdown. She returned to Wellesley to learn that she had been rejected from Frank O'Connor's writing class at Harvard Summer School, to which she had anxiously applied. Already feeling low and exhausted, this news pushed her into a full-blown depression.

Plath decided to spend the summer at home in Wellesley learning shorthand and starting her senior honors thesis on James Joyce's work. But these tasks eluded her. After struggling for several weeks with insomnia and depression, she began cutting herself. Deeply alarmed, Plath's mother brought her to a psychiatrist who prescribed electroshock treatment at Valley Head Hospital in

Carlisle, Massachusetts. There, Plath received a series of outpatient electroshock treatments that were badly administered; these treatments did little to alleviate her depression, which intensified. Terrified of more shock treatments and fearful of a future trapped inside a mental hospital, Plath decided, as she later told Eddie Cohen, to end her life while she still possessed free will and while her family would remember her as a success rather than a mental patient. On August 24, 1953, she left a note on her family dining room table saying she had gone for a walk; she then hid herself in her basement's crawl space and swallowed a bottle of sleeping pills. After three days of frantic searching, her brother found her still alive in the basement.

Plath recovered at a local hospital until Olive Prouty paid for her treatment at McLean, a private psychiatric hospital in Belmont, Massachusetts that catered to wealthy patients. Plath spent September 1953 to early January 1954 at McLean, mainly under the care of Dr. Ruth Beuscher, a young psychiatric resident. Plath was given insulin coma treatment, which made her lethargic, and endured six known electroshock treatments. She was also prescribed Thorazine. Although Dr. Beuscher had earned Plath's trust, Plath dreaded the shock treatments and refused any more after her sixth. Nevertheless, she seemed to respond to the treatment, and was well enough to return to Smith at the start of the spring semester in 1954. She continued to see Dr. Beuscher when she returned home to Wellesley for vacations.

After auditing classes at Smith during her spring 1954 semester, Plath audited Harvard Summer School, eager to prove herself capable of success there. By this time, she had broken up with her boyfriend Dick Norton, and was dating several men, most notably Gordon Lameyer and Richard Sassoon, a French major at Yale with whom she had an intense, literary relationship. Many of her girlfriends at Smith were already engaged, and planned to marry after graduation. Plath resisted an early marriage, convinced she should hold out for a true artistic partner who would respect her professional literary ambitions. Dr. Beuscher had prescribed Plath a diaphragm and during her 1954 summer in Cambridge, she reveled in her newfound sexual freedom, even if that freedom came with risks. She had sex for the first time with a Harvard-educated mathematician and ended up in the ER due to severe hemorrhaging, an episode which inspired a famous scene in *The Bell Jar*. Plath's Smith friend and roommate that summer, Nancy Hunter, was alarmed by what she considered Plath's reckless behavior, but Plath—long incensed about the sexual double standard applied to women—finally felt free to explore her sexuality without fear of pregnancy.

Plath spent the first half of her 1954–5 senior year at Smith writing her honors thesis on the double in Dostoevsky (she had changed her mind about Joyce) titled "The Magic Mirror: A Study of the Double in Two of Dostoevsky's Novels," which her Russian literature professor pronounced a masterpiece. She continued seeing Dr. Beuscher and found time to write more short stories in a class with Alfred Kazin: "The Day Mr. Prescott Died," based on a trip she and her mother had taken to Winthrop to console a grieving family friend; "The Smoky Blue Piano," a light romantic comedy; and "Tongues of Stone," her most accomplished story of 1955. Plath based the story on her experiences at McLean; writing it brought her closer to the themes of *The Bell Jar*. In prose that resembled some of her darkest journal entries, Plath voiced her own experiences of depression and institutionalization:

> she would drag out her nights and days chained to a wall in a dark solitary cell with dirt and spiders . . . she was caught in the nightmare of the body, without a mind, without anything, only the soulless flesh that got fatter with the insulin . . . She had gone on circling at the brink of the whirlpool, pretending to be clever and gay, and all the while these poisons were gathering in her body, ready to break out behind the bright, false bubbles of her eyes at any moment crying: Idiot! Imposter!

The young woman in the story regrets that she had been saved from her first suicide attempt ("They had raised her like Lazarus") and attempts to hang herself, unsuccessfully, in the hospital. The first draft of "Tongues of Stone" ended bleakly, with the protagonist succumbing to the "eternal night" of depression. However, Plath revised the story upon the advice of Alfred Kazin, her writing teacher, and gave it a more hopeful conclusion of recovery. The revised version ends not with the image of night but "the everlasting rising of the sun." This happier ending looks forward to *The Bell Jar*. Plath felt "Tongues of Stone" was "beautifully written" and "the best work of 'art' I've ever done." She was also writing a great amount of poetry under the supervision of her poetry tutor, Alfred Fisher: by the end of her spring semester she had written nearly 50 new poems, enough for a poetry collection, which she assembled in the spring of 1955 and called *Circus in Three Rings*. Plath's confidence grew after *The Atlantic* accepted the collection's title poem, "Circus in Three Rings," that spring.

Despite her suicide attempt, her nearly five months of recovery at McLean Hospital, and her "missed" academic year, Plath was still the star student in Smith's English department. She applied for fellowships to study English literature at various graduate schools, including Oxford, Cambridge, Radcliffe, and Columbia, and eventually won a prestigious Fulbright Fellowship to Newnham College, Cambridge. Plath was ecstatic, and looked forward to a new adventure in England as well as trips to France, Italy, Germany, and Austria. She graduated from Smith in 1955, *summa cum laude*, and sailed to England that September.

The Bell Jar

Many details from Plath's own life—her summer in New York, her breakdown, her suicide attempt, her stay at McLean Hospital, and her relationship with Dick Norton—would inspire scenes in her autobiographical novel *The Bell Jar*. Plath wrote the novel in London, in the spring and possibly summer of 1961 after at least one false start on a novel about her time at Cambridge University. Her experience at St. Pancras Hospital in the spring of 1961, where she recovered from an appendectomy, brought back memories of her earlier hospital stay at McLean, and she began writing *The Bell Jar* quickly after she returned home from the hospital. Likely begun in March, she noted in her journal that she had finished the book by August 22, 1961.

The Bell Jar has become a widely read and taught American novel. But when it was first published in January 1963, the positive but brief reviews, which focused on the heroine's breakdown, did not suggest it would become an international bestseller. Two New York publishers, Alfred A. Knopf and Harper & Row, rejected it in December 1962 and January 1963, respectively. These rejections were a great blow that caused Plath much unhappiness in the weeks before her suicide. The novel was originally marketed as a lurid college girl suicide story: one of Plath's original titles, in fact, was "Diary of a Suicide." It would take years for the book's more subversive and political themes to reveal themselves, and make an impact.

The plot follows a young woman, Esther Greenwood, whose personality and experiences bear similarities to Plath's. But *The Bell Jar* is not a memoir. The novel belongs to the coming-of-age literary genre known as the *Bildungsroman*; more specifically, it is a *Künstlerroman*, about the coming-of-age of an artist. Perhaps the most famous 20th-century *Künstlerroman* is James Joyce's 1916 novel *A Portrait of the Artist as a Young Man*, which Plath had read and studied at Smith. Her notes on the novel show she was inspired by the hero, Stephen Dedalus, who refuses to serve his church or nation (his famous "*non serviam*"), and chooses, instead, a life devoted to art. *A Portrait* was an inspirational text for Plath; the influence of Joyce, who is Esther's thesis topic, is clear throughout the novel. But if *The Bell Jar* is meant to be a portrait of the artist as a young woman, it is an ironic one: Plath shows her readers how limited Esther's life choices are compared to Stephen's.

After a summer working as an intern for *Ladies' Day* magazine in Manhattan (based on Plath's experience at *Mademoiselle*), Esther returns home to her mother's house where she attempts to learn shorthand and get a head start writing her senior honors thesis on James Joyce's notoriously difficult novel *Finnegans Wake*. Soon Esther is in the midst of a major depressive crisis: she cannot sleep, she cannot read. She attempts suicide with sleeping pills and recovers at a mental hospital, based on McLean, under the care of a sympathetic female psychiatrist named Dr. Nolan, based on Dr. Beuscher. Esther endures several electroshock treatments, first at an outpatient clinic, based on Valley Head, where the treatments are badly administered. Her later rounds of shock treatment, under Dr. Nolan's care, seem to cure Esther's depression, at least temporarily. Still, Esther feels betrayed by Dr. Nolan, who gives her little advance warning before her first shock treatment despite knowing Esther's terror of the procedure.

Punishment by electric shock is a prominent theme in *The Bell Jar*, beginning with the first sentence: "It was a queer, sultry summer, the summer they electrocuted the Rosenbergs, and I didn't know what I was doing in New York." From the outset of the novel, Plath makes a larger political point about conformity, dissidence, and punishment by linking the crimes of Julius and Ethel Rosenberg, who were executed for espionage, to Esther Greenwood's more private subversions. (Indeed, the name Esther Greenwood echoes Ethel Rosenberg's maiden name, Ethel Greenglass.) Plath sympathized with the Rosenbergs, whom she saw as victims of McCarthyist hysteria. She decried their execution in her journal in June 1953:

> There is no yelling, no horror, no great rebellion. That is the appalling thing. The execution will take place tonight; it is too bad that it could not be televised ... so much more realistic and beneficial

than the run-of-the mill crime program. Two real people being executed. No matter. The largest emotional reaction over the United States will be a rather large, democratic, infinitely bored and casual and complacent yawn.

The character of Hilda embodies this American indifference when she announces, "I'm so glad they are going to die."

Esther's drive, brilliance, and unwillingness to marry a man who belittles her artistic ambition mark her out as a nonconformist in Eisenhower's America. For this, she will be punished, as the critic Elaine Showalter has noted. Plath makes the connection between Esther's and the Rosenbergs' dissidence clear when she writes, after Esther's first round of shock treatment, "I wondered what terrible thing it was that I had done." Plath also excoriates paternalism in medicine through the character of Dr. Gordon, a condescending psychiatrist who dismisses Esther's anguish and prescribes a disastrous round of shock treatment. (The mid-1950s, around the time the novel is set, saw an all-time high of 559,000 psychiatric inpatients in America.)

Throughout *The Bell Jar*, Plath asks the reader to ponder the moral sacrifices required to conform in a nation gripped by McCarthyism, sexism, racism, and homophobia. The scene where Esther suffers food poisoning after eating spoiled crabmeat suggests the rot at the heart of consumerist American society: "I had a vision of the celestially white kitchens of *Ladies' Day* stretching into infinity. I saw avocado pear after avocado pear being stuffed with crabmeat and mayonnaise and photographed under brilliant white lights. I saw the delicate, pink-mottled claw meat poking seductively through its blanket of mayonnaise ... Poison."

Just as the deceptively rich food makes Esther sick, Plath asks us to question what role a "sick" society plays in Esther's breakdown. She may have encountered this idea in the work of the cultural critic

Erich Fromm, whom she had read in some of her courses at Smith. Fromm argued in his 1955 book *The Sane Society* that the high rates of depression in affluent nations were indicative of a cultural problem. He wrote that "a whole society can be sick" and posited that those who would not accept "the cultural opiate" of "normalcy" often lost their sanity: "Many psychiatrists and psychologists refuse to entertain the idea that society as a whole may be lacking in sanity. They hold that the problem of mental health in a society is only that of the number of 'unadjusted' individuals, and not that of a possible unadjustment of the culture itself." This idea, in the years before second-wave feminism, may have given Plath the courage to make a proto-feminist point in her novel: that Esther's breakdown might be expected in a society that treats women as objects rather than subjects, and in which women rarely control their own destiny. The fact that Esther's breakdown takes place against the backdrop of a women's fashion magazine that commodifies the female body only furthers Plath's political point. In *The Bell Jar*, Esther thinks, "Fashion blurbs, silver and full of nothing, sent up their fishy bubbles in my brain. They surfaced with a hollow pop." Indeed, one of Plath's Smith College roommates remembered Plath calling her *Mademoiselle* work "artificial and banal." Editing a fashion magazine, Plath seems to have felt, was the literary equivalent of "women's work." The August 1953 issue of *Mademoiselle* on which Plath worked resembles a thick fashion catalog with hardly any literary or editorial content between fashion ads and spreads. When Esther throws her tight, constricting clothes off the roof of the Amazon Hotel—just as Plath had thrown her corsets off the top of the Barbizon Hotel, where she stayed in June 1953—she is freeing herself, both literally and metaphorically, from the constrictions that have limited her life as a woman.

Plath wrote *The Bell Jar* in London almost a decade after the events in Massachusetts and New York that inspired the story took place. By then, Plath had achieved the literary and professional ambitions that had seemed, after her breakdown and suicide attempt in 1953, out of reach. As a writer with a published poetry collection, she could afford to look back on her suicide attempt with detachment and even black humor. But Plath is *not* Esther; indeed Plath is sometimes critical of Esther's decisions. Plath had a sophisticated understanding of the complex narrative strategies—such as stream-of-consciousness, interior monologue, fragmentation, and temporal dissonance—used by modernist writers like Joyce, Eliot, and Woolf. She borrowed themes, too, from Eliot and Joyce, particularly, as Amanda Golden has noted, the idea of "death-in-life" and paralysis that afflicts Esther in New York. Just as Joyce treats the character of Stephen Dedalus with distance and irony, so too does Plath view Esther Greenwood. Ted Hughes wrote, in an unpublished draft of a poem, that Plath once told him that Esther's cruelty toward her mother was supposed to show how "mad" Esther had become. Other scenes in which Esther treats marginalized characters with mockery or cruelty may reflect ironic narrative strategies to show how Esther has been poisoned by her racist and homophobic society, and not necessarily reflective of Plath's actual feelings. Although Plath draws upon her own life experiences in *The Bell Jar*, she made the decision to write a novel, not a memoir. Esther Greenwood is a fictional character.

The ending of *The Bell Jar* is ambiguous: Esther eventually becomes a wife and mother, which is the feminine role her conservative society expects her to fulfill. But she has also written her own story. She has made *herself* the subject in a world that prefers to see women as objects. Despite the pain and struggle Esther endures in the novel, those struggles are buoyed by humor and wit. Plath suggests, in the end, that Esther's ability to control her own narrative and destiny—in a world that had attempted to control *her*—is a triumph.

Chapter 4
Rebirth and resurrection

Cambridge and Ted Hughes

Plath arrived at Newnham College, Cambridge, in October 1955. There, she would spend two years on a Fulbright Fellowship earning a second BA in English Literature. At Newnham, one of Cambridge's few all-women's colleges, Plath lived in a dormitory for foreign students called Whitstead and became friendly with some of its residents. She made few English female friends, but dated several English men during her first term. She was also still seeing Richard Sassoon, who was studying at the Sorbonne in Paris.

At Cambridge, the last British university to confer degrees upon women in 1948, Plath was a second-class citizen. (In 1956 she would publish an article about women's subordinate position at Cambridge in the Oxford student publication *Isis*.) She was doubly patronized as an American: many of her British contemporaries at Cambridge remembered her during this time as an over-excited Yank with gushy mannerisms. She threw herself into extracurriculars like the Amateur Dramatic Club, literary magazines, and the university newspaper *Varsity*, but she was overwhelmed by the range of reading and writing required of her as she prepared for the Tripos exam. Moreover, she found Cambridge's decentralized academic system hard to navigate.

When she published a poem, "Three Caryatids Without a Portico," in the literary magazine *Chequer*, one of Ted Hughes's close friends publicly mocked her neat language (she had used words such as "regal," "serenity," "tranquil," and "grace") in another student publication, *Broadsheet*: "Of the quaint and eclectic artfulness of Sylvia Plath's two poems, my better half tells me 'Fraud, fraud'; but I will not say so; who am I to know how beautiful she may be." This breezy, sexist "review" humiliated Plath. No longer coddled by adoring Smith professors and all too aware of the casual misogyny around her, she began to doubt both her poetic talent and capacity for academic success. She fell into a depression during her first term at Cambridge and began seeing a psychiatrist.

In February of 1956, Plath met Ted Hughes at a raucous university party celebrating the launch of a new poetry magazine called the *Saint Botolph's Review*. The magazine published poetry and prose by Hughes and his friends, Cambridge men who had grown tired of what they saw as the prevailing "genteel" ethos of English poetry popularized by a group of poets loosely known as "The Movement"—Donald Davie, Elizabeth Jennings, John Wain, Philip Larkin, and Kingsley Amis. Most of the Saint Botolph's clique felt proud to be outsiders amongst the upper-class Oxbridge set: Hughes was from West Yorkshire, while his friends were Irish, Scottish, Welsh, and American. Their heroes were W. B. Yeats, Robert Graves, and D. H. Lawrence, and they believed that poetry itself was holy incantation delivered to the poet from unconscious or even otherworldly sources. Graves's book *The White Goddess* was a particularly influential text; Hughes called it "the chief holy book of my poetic conscience." Plath was spellbound when she read Hughes's and his American friend Lucas Myers's poems in the first issue of the *Saint Botolph's Review*, and she became determined to meet them. She was struck by their bold cadences, which she called "tight and packed and supple and blazing." She herself wanted to write less decorously, and she found an aesthetic solution of sorts in Hughes's and Myers's work. She thought their poems were "magnificent," and felt that her own were full of "glib, smug littleness" in comparison. In her journal she wrote, "until I make something tight and riding over the limits of sweet sestinas and sonnets ... they can ingnore [*sic*] me."

Hughes had already graduated from Cambridge but was a frequent visitor to the St. Botolph's Rectory, where Myers lived. Both were at the Cambridge launch party for the *Saint Botolph's Review* on February 25, 1956. After meeting Myers, Plath quickly changed course and found Hughes. Plath's attraction to Hughes, and his to her, was immediate. In her journal, she famously wrote, "Then the worst happened, that big, dark, hunky boy, the only one there huge enough for me, who had been hunching around over women, and whose name I had asked the minute I had come into the room ... came over and was looking hard into my eyes and it was Ted Hughes." Both had been drinking. Plath recited his poem "Fallgrief's Girl-Friends" to him over the music of the jazz band, and Hughes kissed her, snatching her headband and earrings. Plath wrote that when he kissed her again she "bit him long and hard on the cheek, and when we came out of the room, blood was running down his face. His poem, 'I did it, I.' Such violence, and I can see how women lie down for artists. The one man in the room who was as big as his poems, huge, with hulk and dynamic chunks of words; his poems are strong and blasting like a high wind in steel girders. And I screamed in myself, thinking: oh, to give myself crashing, fighting, to you." This would become, perhaps, the most famous first date in literary history.

Plath went home with another man that night, but Hughes had made an impression. "Mad passionate abandon," Plath wrote of Hughes in her calendar the next day. She would later recreate the meeting in her autobiographical short story "Stone Boy With Dolphin," whose language was significantly less triumphant than her operatic journal entry. Plath suggests the story's protagonist endured unsettling, drunken sex with the young man she goes home with after the launch party. She depicts "empty consent" in this story before the term was coined. Linda Wagner-Martin points out that Plath was generally ahead of her time when writing about sex, both here and in *The Bell Jar*, as few American women dared to tackle this subject "explicitly" in the 1950s.

Two days after Plath met Hughes, she wrote a poem, "Pursuit," about what she called "the dark forces of lust" in a new style:

> There is a panther stalks me down:
> One day I'll have my death of him;
>
> ----------------------------------
>
> Insatiate, he ransacks the land
> Condemned by our ancestral fault,
> Crying: blood, let blood be spilt;
> Meat must glut his mouth's raw wound.

Plath sent "Pursuit" to her mother, writing that she was "hypnotized by this poem" with its "simple seductive beauty." In the same letter, she wrote, "I am most scornful of the small preciousness of much of my past work" and that she was "making a shift." Plath was emerging out of her formalist chrysalis, beginning to shed her precise New Critical habits, and writing in a bolder style partly inspired by the wildness and ferocity of the poems she had read in the *Saint Botolph's Review*. But the formal patterns she had mastered in high school and college served her well. Plath never abandoned her lyrical poise.

For all her talk about Hughes, Plath was still in love with Richard Sassoon. She was devastated when she traveled to Paris during her 1956 spring break to find that Sassoon had abandoned her, leaving the city for a trip to Spain. Plath ended up traveling through Europe with her old boyfriend Gordon Lameyer, with whom she quarreled before flying back to London—and to Hughes (Figures 4 and 5). The couple fell deeply in love that spring—Hughes often stayed with Plath at Whitstead—and by May, they were engaged. They married secretly on Bloomsday, June 16, in a Bloomsbury church. After a honeymoon in Benidorm,

4. Sylvia Plath in Paris, 1956.

5. Sylvia Plath in Venice, 1956.

Spain, and a trip to meet Hughes's parents in Heptonstall, Yorkshire, Plath returned to Cambridge alone while Hughes stayed behind at his parents' home. (Plath was worried she would lose her Fulbright Fellowship if college officials learned she was married.) During this time, she finished a story she had begun during her honeymoon in Spain, "The Wishing Box."

The story concerns a woman, Agnes, married to a Hughes-like husband who relays his dreams to her each morning. Agnes begins to resent her husband's superior imaginings, which she calls "works of art." As he tells her about his dream-life with famous poets such as William Blake, Agnes simply "smoldered in silence." Her own dreams become duller, and she begins spending her days listlessly watching television and drinking sherry. The story's ending is melodramatic, yet chilling: Agnes dies by suicide dressed in an evening gown. It is tempting to read this story as an oblique commentary on Plath's own relationship with Hughes, or, at the very least, a dark statement about the ways in which women's dreams—or art—become sidelined in marriage. Yet Plath sent

Hughes the story's plot as she worked on it and Hughes responded enthusiastically. She even apologized to Hughes, in a letter, for "plagiarizing" his "magnificent" dreams. Although Plath emphasized her own distance from Agnes ("poor thing") to Hughes, she admitted that the character was "certainly an aspect of one of my selves now." The tension between husband and wife in the story may reflect the tension Plath and Hughes had experienced during their honeymoon, when the couple had their first major argument. This was not the last short story in which Plath would write darkly about marriage: in "The Fifty-Ninth Bear" (1959), a wife wills a bear to kill her husband, while poems such as "The Other Two," "Dialogue Over a Ouija Board," "The Rabbit Catcher," and "Event," among others, speak to marital tension and dissolution.

When letters for "Mrs. Hughes" began arriving at Newnham, Plath finally confessed her marriage to the college tutor and the Fulbright officials, both of whom congratulated her and allowed her to continue her studies without any penalty. Plath and Hughes moved into a flat in Cambridge near Grantchester Meadows in late 1956, and, while Hughes taught at a local boys' school, Plath completed her final two terms at Cambridge, graduating with a 2.1—the second highest degree. The couple applied themselves unrelentingly to writing when they were not otherwise occupied. Both of them were determined to write a new kind of poetry, in a bolder voice, that would stand apart from what they read in the pages of the British journals.

In April 1957, the couple received the astonishing news that Hughes's poetry manuscript, *The Hawk in the Rain*, had won a major poetry prize sponsored by the YMHA of Manhattan (today known as the 92nd Street Y), and judged by three important poets: Marianne Moore, W. H. Auden, and Stephen Spender. The prize came with publication. A minor controversy ensued when Moore asked Hughes to remove two poems that had slight sexual content. Moore's request gave Plath the chance to defend her and Hughes's Lawrentian ethos in a letter to her mother, in which Plath railed against the "cheap, flat 'new movement poetry', which never commits itself, but talks about and about: the meanings are dull, often superficial 'top-of-the-head' philosophizing, and there is no <u>music</u>, no sense picturing. It is hogwash; not even that good." Plath had surely picked up some of her antipathy toward the Movement from Hughes (she was, after all, the author of "Three Caryatids"), but her desire to abandon artifice predated her time with him. As did her use of bold, arresting imagery. She wrote to her mother about Moore's request:

> We feel, strongly, that to cut these two [poems] out would be to silence a large part of Ted's voice: which is raised against the snide, sneaking, coy weekend-review poets whose sex is in their head, & the prissy abstract poets who don't dare to talk about love in anything but mile-distant abstractions. It is Dylan Thomas, but with a faith & deep religious morality which is also Lawrence (both misunderstood by many blind people).

Three days later, Plath wrote her mother again: "We want logic, but not without blood feeling; music without vague emotion.... They think they can ignore us in their magazines, because we are too disturbing. In a year, the whole picture will be changed." She was not wrong (Figures 6 and 7).

In September 1957 *The Hawk in the Rain* was published by Harper & Brothers in America, and Faber and Faber in England, to great acclaim. Hughes's career was launched, thanks to Plath, who had entered Hughes's manuscript in the contest instead of her own. She told others that his book was more ready for publication than hers, which by now had been through several rounds of revision. Plath would put her husband's work ahead of her own throughout the marriage. She joked in letters that she was Hughes's agent but in fact this was exactly the role—along with personal secretary—she took on. She sent out his manuscripts and kept track of his rejections and acceptances;

6. Sylvia Plath in Heptonstall, West Yorkshire, 1956.

handled his contracts and royalty payments; managed his appointments and correspondence; and scouted for literary contests and prizes he might win. Plath did all of this while writing her own work and doing all the housework and cooking. She would question her sacrifice after Hughes left her in 1962.

In 1957, despite her many international publications and literary prizes, Plath was still vying for real poetic recognition. She told others she was "so happy his book is accepted first," but she too hoped to win a prestigious prize that would lead to her book's publication. Her poetry collection—begun in earnest her senior year at Smith and now called *Two Lovers and a Beachcomber*—was shortlisted for the Yale Younger Poets Prize (previously won by her

The Beacon —   Yorkshire 1956 of the painted flock - Hebden Bridge)

7. Sylvia Plath and Ted Hughes in West Yorkshire, 1956.

rival Adrienne Rich), but would lose to John Hollander in August 1957. The loss disappointed her deeply, and her collection remained unpublished.

In the spring of 1957, Plath's former Smith professor Mary Ellen Chase visited her at Cambridge and invited her to teach three sections of Freshman English at Smith. The position was, as one

Smith professor recalled, "the very bottom of the pecking order," but to Plath it meant professional stability and economic security. Plath accepted the job and in June 1957 the couple traveled to America. After a backyard wedding reception at Plath's home in Wellesley, and a second honeymoon on Cape Cod, the couple moved to an apartment near the Smith campus in Northampton. Plath began teaching at Smith in September 1957.

Northampton, Boston, and the Lowell seminar

Plath did not enjoy teaching, initially; she found class preparation, public speaking, and grading exhausting. Hughes taught creative writing at the nearby University of Massachusetts in Amherst during the spring 1958 semester, and found the work surprisingly fulfilling. But he, too, was adamant that teaching killed his creative energy. Teaching left Plath almost no time to write, and she soon decided that she would not return to Smith for a second year. Hughes had received full-time job offers from several local colleges, but he had no intention of remaining in academia. The success of *The Hawk in the Rain*, and the literary friendships the couple had made during their sporadic forays into Boston, gave them confidence that they could support themselves as freelance writers in that city.

In the spring semester of 1958, Plath audited a modern art course at Smith that resulted in eight new poems in a little over a week. She felt it was an aesthetic turning point, and wrote her mother that "the art of primitives like Henri Rousseau, Gauguin and Paul Klee and DeChirico [*sic*]" was her "deepest source of inspiration." These artists led her to break out of what she called her "rococo crystal cage"—another iteration of the poetic "glass caul" in which she felt confined. Her new poems, she thought, were "thunderous," her best work yet. Plath's confidence and enthusiasm about this new turn speaks to the profound effect of modern art on her poetry and sensibility. The Italian painter Giorgio de Chirico was a particularly important influence: Plath told the BBC that her 1957 poem, "The Disquieting Muses," was directly influenced by de Chirico's abstract, surrealist painting of the same title featuring "three terrible, faceless dressmakers' dummies in classical gowns, seated and standing in a weird, clear light." Plath grafted elements of fairytale and surrealism onto this scene. These three "muses" overshadow the speaker's life despite her mother's attempts to drive them away ("witches always, always | Got baked into gingerbread"). The muses are an oblique metaphor of depression, their blank faces both foreign and familiar: "Day now, night now, at head, side, feet, | They stand their vigil in gowns of stone." The speaker, however, will not "betray the company I keep" to her mother. The poem speaks to the shadows and stigma of mental illness, and, perhaps, the role that stigma had played in Plath's complicated relationship with her own mother.

Plath was joyful about her first *New Yorker* acceptances in June 1958 for "Mussel Hunter at Rock Harbor" and "Nocturne." The former poem, written in a precise syllabic style typical of Marianne Moore, was one of Plath's great middle-period successes: in stanzas of seven lines comprising seven syllables, Plath achieves a powerful imagistic rendering of a dead crab, washed ashore, that survives ("saved | Face") its own demise to become art. "Mussel Hunter at Rock Harbor" is a nature poem, but it is also about the artist's power to transform its subject, through observation and compassion, into a rich symbol at odds with nature's cold indifference. During the spring and summer of 1958, Plath wrote two other important poems that were among the most successful of this period. "Lorelei," written in spare, a-b-a tercets, was based on folk tales of the German Rhine maidens she had heard as a child; the poem ends darkly, and somewhat romantically, on an image of suicide: "Stone, stone, ferry me down there." In "Full Fathom Five," an elegy for her father that foreshadowed her later paternal elegies "Electra on Azalea Path," "The Colossus," and "Daddy," Plath also uses water imagery to suggest the depths of emotion in the grieving daughter who walks "dry on your kingdom's border | Exiled to no good." Plath was so pleased with this poem and its references to Shakespeare's *The Tempest* that she changed the name of her poetry collection from *The Earthenware Head* (her previous favorite poem) to *Full Fathom Five*. She wrote in her journal that the title "relates more richly to my life and imagery than anything else I've dreamed up, the association of the sea, which is a central metaphor for my childhood, my poems and the artist's subconscious, to the father image—relating to my own father, the buried male muse & god-creator risen to be my mate in Ted, to the sea-father Neptune—and the pearls and coral highly wrought to art: pearls sea-changed from the ubiquitous grit of sorrow and dull routine." Indeed all three of these poems dealt, in different ways, with grief, and sounded a new, more personal note for Plath.

After a listless summer in Northampton, Plath and Hughes moved to Boston's Beacon Hill in September 1958. In Boston, the couple made important friends and literary connections. Through Jack Sweeney, head of Harvard's Lamont Poetry Room, and Plath's old friend Peter Davison, they met the writers Bill Merwin, Adrienne Rich, Robert Lowell, Elizabeth Hardwick, Robert Frost, Stanley Kunitz, Anne Sexton, Maxine Kumin, John Holmes, and others. Plath saw more of her Smith and Wellesley friends as well, most of whom were now married with children. Despite more opportunities for literary socializing—something she had longed for at Cambridge—she felt stymied by a writing block that fall as she worked on her novel, provisionally titled *Falcon Yard*. Seeking a stabilizing routine, she found a part-time job as a secretary at the outpatient psychiatric clinic at Boston's Massachusetts General Hospital.

It was during this time that Plath wrote what is widely considered to be her most successful short story, "Johnny Panic and the Bible of Dreams," about a young woman working in a psychiatric outpatient clinic who collects patients' dreams. The story has a menacing undertone: when the narrator's "bible of dreams" is discovered by the senior staff, she is punished with electric shock treatment. Plath's description of the procedure is surreal and dystopian, and borrows elements from religion, horror, and science fiction. These effects heighten the atmosphere of terror:

> The crown of wire is placed on my head, the wafer of forgetfulness on my tongue. The masked priests move to their posts and take hold....At the moment when I think I am most lost the face of Johnny Panic appears in a nimbus of arc lights on the ceiling overhead. I am shaken like a leaf in the teeth of glory....The air crackles with his blue-tongued lightning-haloed angels.
>
> His love is the twenty-storey leap, the rope at the throat, the knife at the heart.
>
> He forgets not his own.

The story was based on Plath's experience working at Massachusetts General Hospital, and her own nightmarish shock treatments at Valley Head Hospital in 1953. But she also leans heavily on surrealist techniques in the story; some sequences seem dream-like. Plath called the story "queer and quite slangy," and, perhaps due to its taboo subject, it was rejected by *The Sewanee Review* in 1961. "Johnny Panic" was a continuation of themes she had explored in "Tongues of Stone," and foreshadowed the later mental hospital sections in *The Bell Jar*—particularly the harrowing scenes of Esther's electroshock treatment. The hospital job, which brought back painful memories, did not last long. Plath eventually left for a part-time position as a secretary in the Department of Sanskrit and Indian Studies at Harvard.

In February 1959, Plath decided to attend Robert Lowell's creative writing workshop at Boston University. Plath had likely learned about it from Anne Sexton at a mid-February party hosted by the poet and Tufts professor John Holmes, and whose guests included Plath, Hughes, Sexton, Robert Lowell, Maxine Kumin, Stanley Kunitz, and other local poets. In Lowell's workshop, Plath befriended Sexton, an affluent mother of two (also originally from Wellesley) who suffered from depression and substance abuse, and who had been hospitalized for previous suicide attempts. Sexton did not have a college education, and had embarked upon a career as a poet after finding some success in an adult education creative writing class taught by Holmes. Talented, glamorous, and flamboyant, she had impressed Lowell enough to audit his seminar in 1958. Lowell and Sexton were writing a new kind of poetry, later dubbed "confessionalism," and their influence helped loosen Plath's line. At Smith, as we have seen, Plath had written tidy, meticulously executed poetry. Her voice and rhythms began to change slightly after she met Hughes, with poems like "Pursuit." Still, she struggled to break out of her "glass caul," especially during her Boston year. She read part of Lowell's seminal collection, *Life Studies*—with its intimate portraits of family dysfunction, mental illness, and breakdown—before it was published in April 1959. She also read Sexton's searing poem, "The Double Image," about the poet's mental illness and difficult relationship with her mother. Such themes resonated with Plath, who had addressed her own experiences with mental illness, asylums, and suicide in her fiction but not in her poetry.

Life Studies was widely praised when it was published in the spring of 1959, as was Sexton's first collection, *To Bedlam and Part Way Back* (1960). Later, in a 1962 interview, Plath acknowledged how powerful Lowell's and Sexton's examples had been, calling *Life Studies* an "intense breakthrough into very serious, very personal, emotional experience" and Sexton's work, with its attention to motherhood and mental illness, full of "emotional and psychological depth" that was "quite new, quite exciting." Lowell's and Sexton's example—and success—gave Plath creative permission to write more openly in her poems about subjects that had previously seemed off-limits. Plath was likely influenced, too, by the emotions she was analyzing in her therapy sessions with Dr. Beuscher, which she had resumed in late 1958. She wrote a friend, "I am leaving the rather florid over-metaphorical style that encrusted me in college. The 'Feminine' (horrors) lavish coyness. The poems I have written this year are, if anything, 'ugly.'" Among those poems were "Electra on Azalea Path," which was an elegy for Otto (she visited his grave for the first time in spring 1959), "Suicide Off Egg Rock," and "Man in Black." In "Electra on Azalea Path," Plath wrote, "I am the ghost of an infamous suicide, | My own blue razor rusting in my throat.... || It was my love that did us both to death."

Meanwhile, Hughes wrote the poems of his second collection, *Lupercal.* Plath still struggled to find a publisher.

Yaddo, "The Colossus," and "Poem for a Birthday"

After a summer driving across Canada and America to visit Plath's relatives in California, Plath and Hughes decamped to Yaddo, the renowned artists' colony in Saratoga Springs, New York. They spent the fall of 1959 writing and taking long walks through the woodsy, cloistered grounds. At Yaddo, Plath and Hughes had their own separate writing studios; the physical distance from both the outside world and her husband served Plath well. She was finally free to write without managing the daily domestic grind of cooking and cleaning. Plath, who was pregnant and in her second trimester that fall, wrote her mother that she had never "felt so peaceful and as if I can read and think and write for about 7 hours a day." Yet Plath experienced a resurgence of depression and panic at Yaddo, which she called "the old fall disease." The publisher Henry Holt rejected her poetry manuscript in October, while both Knopf and Harcourt, Brace rejected two children's books she had written, *The It-Doesn't-Matter Suit* and *The Bed Book.* These three rejections hit her very hard. She wrote in her journal that October, "Very depressed today. Unable to write a thing. Menacing gods. I feel outcast on a cold star, unable to feel anything but an awful helpless numbness.... My shaping spirit of imagination is far from me."

Hughes advised her to start a new poetry collection. She took his advice, and, at Yaddo, she experienced a stylistic and thematic breakthrough with her poems "The Colossus," "The Manor Garden," and "Poem for a Birthday." The Harvard poetry critic Helen Vendler felt "The Colossus" was Plath's first important mature poem. In it, Plath mocks the genteel poetic language she had become so adept at using, and instead writes something, as she would have put it, uglier. The poem's speaker, who tends her father's monument on a faraway island, is lonely and embittered by her caretaking role, yet unable to relinquish it and abandon the father's corpus to rot and ruin: "Thirty years now I have labored | To dredge the silt from your throat. | I am none the wiser." The metaphor is clear: subservience to "the Father," whether that be literal or ideological, strands women on their own islands of isolation and neglect. Plath even takes subversive aim at the language of patriarchy when she writes that the father's language—"Mule-bray, pig-grunt and bawdy cackles"—sounds "worse than a barnyard." This point is especially pertinent given that the poem draws upon Shakespeare's *The Tempest*, Swift's *Gulliver's Travels*, and Defoe's *Robinson Crusoe*. The mocking, taunting, authority-flouting voice that propelled later triumphs like "Lady Lazarus" and "Daddy" is on its first full display here. "Perhaps you consider yourself an oracle," Plath writes dismissively, "some god or other." But the dutiful daughter resigns herself to her exile—and continual servitude—at the end of the poem.

Plath's other poetic triumph from the Yaddo period was the "Poem for a Birthday" sequence, which grew out of a poetic exercise Plath and Hughes had embarked upon. After exploring Yaddo's greenhouse during her birthday week in late October 1959, Plath wrote what she called "a series of madhouse poems." She drew upon surrealist imagery as she attempted to depict the process of breakdown and rebirth: "Let me sit in a flowerpot, | The spiders won't notice. | My heart is a stopped geranium." In "The Stones," the final poem in the sequence, Plath conjures an assembly line of "spare parts" and workmen who help to put the suffering speaker back together again ("I shall be good as new"). Hughes felt "The Stones" was Plath's finest Yaddo poem, and the first time he heard Plath's "real" poetic voice. Yet this voice was so strongly influenced by the poet Theodore Roethke that when Plath later tried to publish "Poem for a Birthday" in the Knopf edition of her first collection, *The Colossus*, the poet Stanley Kunitz advised its removal on the grounds that Plath had practically plagiarized Roethke's poem "The Lost Son." Still, Plath knew she had broken new ground at Yaddo and had been true, as she wrote in her journal, to her own "weirdnesses." Even as she worried that she had not successfully demolished the "drawingroom [*sic*] inhibitions" in her short stories, she knew she had done so in her poems: "There I have." That October she received a letter from a young editor, James Michie, at the British publisher Heinemann (D. H. Lawrence's publisher) that confirmed her growing confidence: Michie praised recent poems she had published in *The London Magazine*, and asked her to send him her unpublished poetry collection.

England, motherhood, and *The Colossus*

Plath and Hughes had already decided, in mid-1959, that they would return to England at year's end. Hughes had grown increasingly disenchanted with life in America, and felt himself an exile—though the experience of living abroad had been good for his poetry. Plath was also ready for a new chapter, and had been persuaded to move to England by their friend Bill Merwin's stories of regular, high-paying commissions from the BBC and free health care from the NHS. (Plath's baby was due in late March.) Plath and Hughes knew that if they stayed in America, they would have to support themselves by teaching—an occupation both found harmful to their creative drive and literary aspirations.

The couple returned to England in December 1959 and, after a cramped stint with Hughes's parents in Yorkshire, moved to a small flat overlooking a charming square in north London. Plath enjoyed life in London, where Hughes was now something of a literary celebrity, and she made several close female friends in the city. Michie, the editor who had contacted her at Yaddo, soon wrote accepting her poetry manuscript, now titled *The Colossus*. Plath signed the contract at a pub in Soho, then celebrated her success with Hughes over champagne.

Frieda Rebecca Hughes was born on April 1, 1960, around the same time that Hughes's second collection *Lupercal* was published to rave reviews. Hughes's reputation soared—he appeared in a photograph in the *Sunday Times* alongside W. H. Auden, T. S. Eliot, Stephen Spender, and Louis MacNeice at a Faber and Faber party—while Plath adjusted to her new role as mother. She continued to write: poems she finished that summer included "Sleep in the Mojave Desert," "Two Campers in Cloud Country," "The Hanging Man," and "Stillborn." These were dark poems, tinged with menace; the imagery of "The Hanging Man," for example, suggests Plath's terrible experience with electroshock therapy in its devastating couplets: "By the roots of my hair some god got hold of me. | I sizzled in his blue volts like a desert prophet." Time was in short supply as she cared for the new baby, did nearly all the housework, and continued to act as Hughes's agent and secretary. She felt she was helping his career, and by extension her own. Indeed, by the summer of 1960 the couple was dining with T. S. Eliot.

The Colossus was published on October 31, 1960. The book contained only three poems Plath had written in or before 1956; the poems she had chosen for the final cut were less formal, cerebral, and playful than those she had included in earlier versions of the collection. The language was darker, and the lines somewhat looser; the spirit of the collection was Romantic rather than Metaphysical. Plath's aesthetic instincts were good, for these were more achieved poems than most of what she had written at Smith and Cambridge. The strongest poems in the book included "The Colossus," "Full Fathom Five," "Mussel Hunter at Rock Harbor," "The Stones," "The Manor Garden," and "Lorelei."

The Colossus received excellent reviews from prominent writers and critics in major literary publications. *Poetry* magazine noted that Plath wanted "to make you *hear* what she sees, the texture of her language affording a kind of analogue for the experience she presents." Al Alvarez, the most important young poetry critic in England, gave the book an outstanding review in the *Observer*, though his language suggests the sexism Plath had to overcome to be taken seriously as a woman poet: "She steers clear of feminine charm, deliciousness, gentility, supersensitivity and the act of being a poetess. She simply writes good poetry." Alvarez picked up on the sense of "menace" that propelled some of Plath's language, "that gives her work its distinction." On the next page, as if confirming the strength of Plath and Hughes's poetic partnership, Alvarez declared Hughes's *Lupercal* the best poetry book of the year. Shortly after these triumphant reviews, in January 1961, Plath and Hughes gave a BBC talk titled "Poets in Partnership," in which both discussed the advantages, and minor annoyances, of their creative marriage. But the cracks in the marriage's foundation—Plath and Hughes had married after only two full months of continuous dating—were beginning to show.

Plath suffered a miscarriage in February 1961 following what she described to her psychiatrist in a 1962 letter as a physical fight with Hughes. The harrowing incident prompted a bitter aesthetic turn—Plath wrote the poem "Zoo Keeper's Wife," with its acidic and mocking tone ("I entered your bible, I boarded your ark"), shortly after her miscarriage: "Old grievances jostling each other, so many loose teeth. | But what would you know about

that | My fat pork, my marrowy sweetheart, face-to-the-wall?"
It was the first mature poem Plath wrote in the voice of a
wronged woman, but it would not be her last. Just a few weeks
after her miscarriage, Plath wrote her groundbreaking
poem "Parliament Hill Fields" about this traumatic experience
("I suppose it's pointless to think of you at all. | Already your doll
grip lets go"). Plath bravely confronted an entrenched societal
taboo when she read this poem aloud on the BBC that June,
with an introduction that made the poem's subject clear. She
also wrote another enduring poem about motherhood that
February, "Morning Song," with its famous first line, "Love set
you going like a fat gold watch." The poem is celebratory, yet it
does not sentimentalize the experience of motherhood. None of
Plath's poems on this subject would. Her attitude is more
existential: "I'm no more your mother | Than the cloud that
distills a mirror to reflect its own slow | Effacement at the
wind's hand."

Plath underwent an appendectomy that spring, an experience
which inspired one of her best poems, "Tulips." Hughes
remembered that "Tulips" marked a turning point for Plath; it was
the first poem that he saw her write without using her thesaurus.
The poem's speaker, recovering from an illness in a hospital ward,
describes her ambivalence about returning home to her family
responsibilities (she describes a photograph of her husband and
child as "little smiling hooks"), and her desire for stasis: "I only
wanted | To lie with my hands turned up and be utterly empty."
Plath describes the speaker's inertia and loss of identity as
pleasurable, almost sensuous:

> Look how white everything is, how quiet, how snowed-in.
> I am learning peacefulness, lying by myself quietly
> As the light lies on these white walls, this bed, these hands.
> I am nobody; I have nothing to do with explosions.
> I have given my name and my day-clothes up to the nurses
> And my history to the anesthetist and my body to the surgeons.

A vase of bright red tulips on her bedside table, however, disturbs this deathly peace: they are "too red in the first place, they hurt me." Their heady color and scent draw her out of her numbness almost against her will. The tulips' beauty breaks through her inertia, and the poem ends as the speaker weeps, restored to health and self-love. The fact that the speaker is a mother should not be overlooked; here Plath speaks obliquely to the physical and emotional toll of motherhood, and the loss of self that caretaking sometimes engenders. In the hospital, others care for the mother-speaker—an experience so rare, she suggests, that she longs to remain in the limbo of recovery. If the poem is about a wish for oblivion, Plath also points to the gendered circumstances which would make an exhausted wife and mother reluctant to return home; in this sense, "Tulips," like "Parliament Hill Fields," confronts a maternal taboo. Plath's own mother explained her understanding of the poem to Olive Prouty: "after major surgery, I just floated thankfully, yet in clouded consciousness, reluctant to take up the business of full return to living."

Plath's hospital stay inspired another major poem, "In Plaster," about a patient recovering in a full body cast. The poem's speaker-patient inhabits the "old yellow" body imprisoned beneath the clean alabaster cast, which the speaker describes as "superior" and "one of the real saints." "I shall never get out of this! There are two of me now," Plath writes. Plath here explores the "double" theme that had fascinated her since her Smith days, when she had written a thesis about the double in Dostoyevsky's work. The poem expresses a divided condition that Plath knew well, and which would have been familiar to many women in 1961. The plaster cast represents the "outer" self that conformed to conservative standards of femininity dictated by society. This self is at odds with the more authentic "inner" self that secretly rebels from such strictures. In the poem, the speaker's cast—a literal bodily prison—is a metaphor for the societal repressions that keep women's true emotions and desires encased. The cast, Plath says, "was shaped just the way I was" but was "unbreakable and with no

59

complaints." It represents the perfect, selfless woman who sacrifices her own desires to serve others. Plath makes this role explicit when she calls the cast "the best of nurses," full of "tidiness," "calmness," and "patience." The speaker within the cast, on the other hand, is none of these things: she is "ugly and hairy," with "habits" that offend. The speaker trapped within feels increasingly claustrophobic: "Living with her was like living with my own coffin."

The emotional toll of living a divided life, especially as an ambitious woman in the 1950s and 1960s, is on full display in this witty but unsettling poem. This theme had a prominent place in the novel Plath was about to begin: *The Bell Jar*. Indeed, Hughes later suggested, in an unpublished poem, that "In Plaster" was the key to understanding the character of Esther Greenwood and even the *Ariel* poems that followed:

> There you are: Prisoner & Jailor,
> Perfectly parabled.
> And for the first time (not quite the first)
> The prisoner speaks the speech
> And stays centre-stage
> The jailor, no more voice than a straitjacket
> Dangling on a tree, never after
> Got a word in.

Hughes finished the section, "Ariel was at large." He felt "In Plaster" marked the point that Plath stopped pretending to be the "good girl" that society demanded—a role fiercely at odds with her determination to become a great writer, an ambition that was regarded as self-aggrandizing, even selfish, for a woman at this time. The speaker of "In Plaster" exhibits a steely determination to break free of the saintly façade imposed upon her, and to honor the authentic voice within. This escape was something that Hughes had been encouraging for years, and which Plath herself had been attempting since at least 1959, when she had written in her journal about longing to break free from her "glass caul." She was speaking about shedding her overreliance on poetic form, but encoded within this desire was a more general need to break from similarly "encasing" feminine rules that encouraged self-censorship, subordination, and subservience. These were the rules of a patriarchal society, designed to keep women from becoming great writers—or great leaders of any kind. Such rules kept women powerless and "in their place." Sexton had managed to break through in *To Bedlam and Part Way Back*, which received good reviews from some of the most important poets in America; perhaps this was the point at which Plath did, too. For at the end of "In Plaster," Plath's speaker declares herself victorious: "I'm collecting my strength; one day I shall manage without her."

For years Plath had struggled to finish a novel. Her time in St. Pancras Hospital, and perhaps the experience of writing "In Plaster," broke "the dykes" as she put it: not long after she left the hospital in March 1961, she began writing *The Bell Jar*. Around this time an editor at Knopf, Judith Jones, wrote confirming that Knopf would publish *The Colossus* in America—news that made Plath, who cared deeply about American publication, relieved and happy. She had been working intermittently on her Cambridge novel *Falcon Yard*, but progress was slow. She told a friend she'd had "a terrible block about Writing a Novel" for nearly 10 years, but the news that Knopf had accepted *The Colossus* released "a fearsome excitement" in her. She stayed up all night mapping her new novel's plot. "I've never been so excited about anything." Plath admitted in her journal that her experience at St. Pancras Hospital brought back memories of her earlier stays at Valley Head, Massachusetts General, and McLean. That spring, she worked on *The Bell Jar* in Bill Merwin's study around the corner (he was vacationing in France) from eight to one each morning. She would finish the novel by late August.

Around this time Plath and Hughes began searching for a rural retreat in Devon, where property was more affordable and there was an express train to London. Hughes was ill at ease with his newfound fame, and wanted to move to the countryside where he could fish and write in peace. Plath preferred London, and had hatched various plans to buy a townhouse in her neighborhood, but the prices were out of reach. The couple eventually settled upon a large old manor home called Court Green in the village of North Tawton, Devon, where they moved with Frieda in September of 1961. Plath was again pregnant and due in January.

Chapter 5
"The blood jet is poetry"— Devon, London, and *Ariel*

An American in Devon

At Court Green, Plath had her own private study—finally, a room of her own. The space and solitude benefited her work. But the first poem she wrote there spoke of disintegration rather than fulfillment (Figure 8). In "Wuthering Heights," the speaker, alone on the Yorkshire moors, describes the ruined farmhouse that allegedly inspired Brontë's novel *Wuthering Heights*. Plath and Hughes had made pilgrimages to this site, not far from his family's home in Heptonstall, when they were visiting Yorkshire. Plath had even called herself and Hughes "a happy Heathcliffe [*sic*] and Cathy!" But now she reimagined the scene: "The horizons ring me like faggots, | Tilted and disparate, and always unstable." The sky itself seems "To funnel my heat away." She hears an eerie mantra on the wind: "Black stone, black stone." The farmhouse's physical deterioration becomes a metaphor for the speaker's spiritual or emotional state, though she never specifies what makes her feel suffocated and disoriented. At the poem's end, she is glad to return to the village, a beacon in the dark. The speaker seems aware that her attraction to the lonely ruin and its void is dangerous: "If I pay the roots of the heather | Too close attention, they will invite me | To whiten my bones among them." Lights beckon her to return to community, but the sense of menace lingers. The poem's competing images of home and

8. Court Green as it looks today, North Tawton, Devon.

shelter—one a cold ruin, the other warm and welcoming—suggest Plath's own sense of dislocation as an "exile" twice removed: an American in England, a Londoner in Devon. Plath herself used the word "exile" at one point to describe her situation in North Tawton, and her letters during this period suggest her homesickness. The move to Devon was the culmination of a years-long search for a home of their own, yet Plath found herself cut off from intellectual friends in London. She complained in letters that she missed the presence of other "'college-educated' mothers" with whom she might socialize.

In September and October of 1961, Plath wrote more poems, including "Mirror," "Blackberrying," "Finisterre," "Last Words," "The Babysitters," "The Surgeon at 2 a.m.," and "The Moon and the Yew Tree," the strongest of the group. "The Moon and the Yew Tree" began as an exercise devised by Hughes; Plath was having trouble sleeping one night and he told her to write a poem about what she saw out of their bedroom window, which faced a churchyard and a large yew tree. What began with a casual suggestion resulted in one of Plath's most powerful poems. Plath's extraordinary description of the speaker's mind suggests exile, loneliness, and despair—and, perhaps, the mindscape of depression: "This is the light of the mind, cold and planetary. | The trees of the mind are black. The light is blue." The poem's speaker feels exiled and despondent about her inability to find community. She contemplates the love she might have received from a Christian God, but decides, somewhat forlornly, that "The moon is my mother. She is not sweet like Mary." The speaker thinks about the saints inside the church, "stiff with holiness." But this potential source of solace and belonging is unavailable to the speaker, whose spiritual exile is compounded by her sense of dislocation. Plath writes, "How I would like to believe in tenderness— | The face of the effigy, gentled by candles, | Bending, on me in particular, its mild eyes." In the end, as in the beginning, the speaker finds herself morally and spiritually adrift, resigned to an unrelenting psychic loneliness: "And the message of the yew tree is blackness—blackness and silence."

Plath wrote about similar themes that fall in her short story "Mothers," which also deals with exile and integration. Plath's protagonist, Esther, is an American living in a Devon village and searching for community amongst its women. In the story, the village rector visits Esther and asks if she believes in the power of prayer. Esther says she does, and begins to tear up, thinking to herself, "How I would like to. Later, she wondered if the tears weren't caused by her vision of the vast, irrevocable gap between her faithless state and the beatitude of belief." Plath's poem "The Babysitters," which addresses her close Smith friend Marcia Brown and recalls their summer nannying for wealthy families in Swampscott, Massachusetts, suggests nostalgia for her American past and community. All three of these works, written during Plath's first autumn in Devon, speak to her sense of isolation as she tried to assimilate into a rural, insular English village far from her

London friends (including the poet Ruth Fainlight) and even farther from her close American friends and family. Plath wrote to others during this time that she felt the villagers regarded her and Hughes as "artists and outlanders," though she would eventually become close to the town midwife and another local mother as winter turned to spring.

The couple's perennial money concerns eased somewhat on account of Plath's Eugene Saxton grant and Hughes's BBC work (they would pay off their mortgage on Court Green in December 1961), but Plath still longed to break into the women's magazine market. She had not published a short story in a woman's magazine since 1953's "Initiation" in *Seventeen*. This dry spell upset her, and she signed with a London agent hoping to crack the British women's magazine market. In 1961 she published "My Perfect Place" in *My Weekly*, a sentimental story in which the female protagonist breaks her engagement with a financially secure fiancé to pursue a brooding artist. But Plath's goal was the American magazine market, which paid handsomely; she knew prose could subsidize the less lucrative practice of poetry. She sent formulaic stories to British and American magazines, and most were rejected. She had an easier time publishing poems in *The New Yorker*, which had given her a coveted first reading contract. She enjoyed putting together a poetry selection for the *Critical Quarterly* supplement *American Poetry Now*, which distracted her from Heinemann's concerns about libel issues in *The Bell Jar*. (She would publish the novel under a pseudonym, Victoria Lucas.) She was also growing increasingly alarmed after reading political articles in *The Nation* about the prospect of nuclear war. Hughes later said that the reason they chose to live in Devon was on account of a map he and Plath had consulted bearing the locations of nuclear waste dumps. Devon, they determined, was "upwind" of any potential fallout from a nuclear strike or accident.

That winter, Plath wrote a short but powerful essay, "Context," published in *The London Magazine* in February 1962. In it she spoke of "fallout," the Military Industrial complex, and political violence in Algeria. Did these realities affect the kind of poetry she wrote? "Yes, but in a sidelong fashion.... My poems do not turn out to be about Hiroshima, but about a child forming itself finger by finger in the dark. They are not about the terrors of mass extinction, but about the bleakness of the moon over a yew tree in a neighboring graveyard." Consciously or not, Plath was addressing the charges of solipsism inherent in writing confessional poetry. Her poetry, she wrote, was not an "escape" from horrific geopolitical realities, but rather a "deflection." She sought to write about universal themes of "hurt and wonder," love, children, the longing for peace. Plath suggests here that poems should not be overtly political any more than they should be overtly personal: both wilt quickly. She singled out the work of Robert Lowell, Theodore Roethke, Elizabeth Bishop, and Stevie Smith for praise, ending, "Surely the great use of poetry is its pleasure—not its influence as religious or political propaganda." Plath makes a strong case for the poem as an aesthetic artifact rather than a vehicle for political change, though the work she was writing around this time eschewed traditionally "beautiful" or sentimental tropes. Her sense that poems ought to give "pleasure" helps explain her adherence to strict formal structures in the radical poems she would write later that year, such as "Daddy" and "Lady Lazarus."

Plath gave birth to a boy, Nicholas, in mid-January 1962. With the care of two children, she had less time to write, but she was determined to use her experience of childbirth and motherhood in her work. In March, she wrote an extraordinary verse play called "Three Women," inspired by the 1958 Ingmar Bergman film *So Close to Life*, which followed the experiences of three mothers in a maternity ward. "Three Women" was the work Anne Stevenson called "the first great poem of childbirth in the language." Indeed, "Three Women" was Plath's first overtly feminist work. It addressed childbirth, miscarriage, adoption, abortion, post-partum depression, and the general anxiety that attends motherhood through the "Voices" of three mothers.

First Voice belongs to the mother who most closely resembles Plath herself; she gives birth to a healthy son but worries about her ability to shield him from the world's physical and emotional dangers: "How long can I be a wall, keeping the wind off? | How long can I be | Gentling the sun with the shade of my hand, | Intercepting the blue volts of a cold moon?" Second Voice is that of an office worker who has a miscarriage, but, because of societal taboo, is not allowed to grieve publicly. She is forced into silence, furious at the men who control women's lives and, Plath suggests, their narratives. "Governments, parliaments, societies, | The faceless faces of important men." She calls them "jealous gods."

Third Voice is that of a university student who gives her baby up for adoption. In the wake of this brutal decision, she addresses the men who dare to judge her for her pregnancy out of wedlock and her contemplation of abortion: "And what if they found themselves surprised, as I did? | They would go mad with it." The speaker is all too aware that her decision to give up her baby is not necessarily a free one in a society that ostracizes single, unmarried mothers. But she also knows "I wasn't ready," and makes her fateful choice: "She is a small island, asleep and peaceful, | And I am a white ship hooting: Goodbye, goodbye." (Third Voice was likely influenced by Anne Sexton's "Unknown Girl in the Maternity Ward," published in 1960's *To Bedlam and Part Way Back*.) "Three Women," which was eventually broadcast on the BBC in 1962, was radical in its unsentimental depiction of childbirth and motherhood.

Plath was beginning to tear away the veil of propriety—what Al Alvarez called "gentility" in his influential 1962 anthology *The New Poetry*—to reveal those parts of women's experience that were left unspoken, or silenced. This was a thematic move which began with "The Colossus," when she mocked the father's language as a series of barnyard grunts. This "other voice" revealed itself again in "Zoo Keeper's Wife." Now Plath found herself mastering this darker, authoritative voice in poems like "The Moon in the Yew Tree," "Three Women," and "Elm." In "Elm," she drew upon experiences from her own suicide attempt and shock treatment to create a voice that personified depression. The poem, which Plath dedicated to Ruth Fainlight and wrote over the course of several drafts in April 1962, begins, "I know the bottom, she says." It returns to themes Plath had first written about in "Mary Ventura and the Ninth Kingdom"—the petrification of will, and the temptation of suicide. Plath writes, in "Elm," of that deadly directive: "I am terrified by this dark thing | That sleeps in me; | All day I feel its soft, feathery turnings, its malignity." The poem ends as the speaker glimpses a "murderous" face in the elm. "It petrifies the will. These are the isolate, slow faults | That kill, that kill, that kill." Plath would use this voice to bracing effect in *Ariel*.

Loss of Eden

In May 1962, Plath and Hughes hosted Assia and David Wevill at Court Green for a weekend. Assia was a German-Israeli advertising copywriter; her husband David was a poet. The Hugheses had sublet their London flat to the Wevills, with whom they felt a literary kinship, and had since stayed in touch. Hughes and Assia embarked upon an affair during that May weekend at Court Green. Plath was devastated, and wrote her former psychiatrist Ruth Beuscher a series of long, searing letters in which she laid bare both her anger toward Hughes and her fear of losing him. Plath wrote "Event" and "The Rabbit Catcher" in May, shortly after the Wevills' visit to Court Green, about a partnership in trouble. The material in the poems reflected the dark turn in her own marriage. In "Event," Plath writes mournfully, "Love cannot come here," "Who has dismembered us?," and "We touch like cripples." In "The Rabbit Catcher," Plath characterizes a Hughes-like figure as a ruthless predator:

And we, too, had a relationship—
Tight wires between us,
Pegs too deep to uproot, and a mind like a ring
Sliding shut on some quick thing,
The constriction killing me also.

Plath sent Alvarez these two poems, as well as "Elm," for publication in the *Observer*. He responded enthusiastically to all three, and Plath began to see him as a new professional ally and sounding-board in the midst of her volatile breakup with Hughes. Indeed, the thinly veiled personal subject matter of these poems upset Hughes, who was surprised to find the drama of his unraveling marriage suddenly made public.

Around this time, Plath burned the manuscript of her second novel, *Falcon Yard*, about her Cambridge years, her love for Hughes, and her new life in Devon. It was to be a sequel to *The Bell Jar*, but told, according to Aurelia, through "the eyes of health." Aurelia witnessed Plath burning the novel in a bonfire at Court Green after Plath learned of Hughes's infidelity. She told her mother it was the funeral pyre of all her hopes and dreams. Plath began planning a new, darker novel, initially titled *The Interminable Loaf*, and later, *Doubletake*, and finally *Double Exposure*. Few details are known about this novel, which disappeared, apparently half-finished at the time of Plath's death. Plath told Olive Prouty that it was to be about Hughes's betrayal, and wrote to the wife of Hughes's painter friend, Barrie Cooke, that the husband figure in the novel, based on Hughes, was a painter. Assia Wevill (one of the few known to have read it) was disturbed to find that Plath had turned her into an unattractive caricature; Bill Merwin's wife Dido was also pilloried. The Plath figure herself, Assia told a friend, was full of "kicks and kids." Olwyn Hughes also read this work after Plath's death, and said parts had contained a play-by-play version of the May weekend when the Wevills had visited Court Green.

Plath was ill with flu much of that summer of 1962, and her weight dropped dangerously low. She was also deeply upset by a letter from the poet Marianne Moore to her Knopf editor calling her poems "bitter, frost-bitten, burnt out, averse." Hughes was often in London with Assia, and Plath had to rely on friends to help care for her and the children. By late August, she wrote her mother, she had made a decision to separate from Hughes. Distracted by grief and laid low by illness, Plath wrote only one poem that month, "Burning the Letters," inspired by the letters from Assia to Hughes that she had found in his study and burned:

> And here is an end to the writing,
> The spry hooks that bend and cringe, the smiles, the smiles.
> And at least it will be a good place now, the attic.
> At least I won't be strung just under the surface,
> Dumb fish

Plath later told a friend that her life with Hughes and the children at Court Green, before Assia, was a lost Eden.

Anne Sexton's newest poetry collection, *All My Pretty Ones*, arrived in Plath's post that summer. Plath wrote to Sexton immediately, full of praise for her poems. "I was absolutely stunned and delighted with the new book." She called it "superbly masterful, womanly in the greatest sense, and so blessedly unliterary. One of the rare and original things in this world one comes upon." Sexton's influence on Plath's 1962–3 poems has been much discussed; indeed, Plath herself gave Sexton a list of her favorites ("The Black Art" topped her list). The poems of *All My Pretty Ones* and Lowell's *Life Studies* encouraged Plath in a direction she was already moving—away from the decorous mannerisms, intricate formalism, and veiled meanings of her Smith and Cambridge poems, and closer to the direct authoritative voice and emotional honesty of poems like "Elm" and "The Moon in the Yew Tree." Alvarez had encouraged this direction as well in *The New Poetry*, in which he railed against the complacency of

English gentility and the limited world view of the poetry it engendered. This was also an aesthetic transformation that Hughes had encouraged since their earliest days as a couple. But Plath's "new" voice was distinctly her own, and could not be called "confessional." Her poems were still full of myth, symbol, and surrealism that distorted autobiographical elements; the self-reflection in these poems was that of a funhouse mirror. While she depicted emotions such as heartbreak, anger, despondency, and love with direct precision—Plath's speakers no longer look away—she divulged little specific, personal information.

Plath continued to write to Dr. Beuscher throughout the summer of 1962 as her mood and weight dropped. She still hoped, despite the terrible events of the past few months, that she and Hughes might reconcile. To that end, the couple journeyed to the west of Ireland in September 1962, where they stayed with the poet Richard Murphy and visited Yeats sites at Coole Park and Thoor Ballylee. The trip achieved not a reconciliation but a permanent sundering: Hughes decamped to Barrie Cooke's house in County Clare near the end of the trip, leaving Plath to travel by train and ferry back to Devon alone. Murphy had encouraged her to get a divorce rather than a separation, and shortly after arriving home, she began the legal process to do so.

The October poems

Hughes left Court Green for good on October 11, 1962. His absence plunged Plath into a period of emotional volatility and creative inspiration. She would write nearly all of her best-known poems of *Ariel* during the months of September, October, and November 1962, a historic outpouring that rivals that of John Keats in its intensity and speed. During this time, she wrote nearly as many poems as she had written in the two previous years. As Plath wrote Ruth Fainlight in London, "I kept telling myself I was the sort that could only write when peaceful at heart, but that is not so, the muse has come to live, now that Ted is gone, and my God! what a sweeter companion." Hughes's leave-taking seemed to release something in Plath. As she wrote to Bill Merwin, "All I want is my own life—not to be anybody's wife, but to be free to travel, move, work, be without check." Plath channeled her heartbreak and anger into her work, riding the waves of her fury at Hughes. She wrote to others repeatedly about her hope for a new, independent life. The future began to look brighter. Plath knew she was capable of producing first-rate poems and fiction; the real challenge was finding stable, steady childcare. The arrival of a young, capable (one of Plath's highest compliments), and enthusiastic nanny, Susan O'Neill-Roe, allowed Plath more time to write that fall. Sue was good with the children, and good company for Plath.

Plath's literary hero James Joyce had created a character, Stephen Dedalus, in *A Portrait of the Artist as a Young Man* who refused to serve the national and religious institutions he felt would kill his artistic spirit. This was, in Joyce's memorable phrase, Stephen's *non serviam*. We might think of *Ariel* as Plath's *non serviam*, for in these poems, Plath rejected the anodyne, decorous constraints on language that she felt had limited women poets before her. In "The Tour," for example, written in late October, the speaker flaunts her messy house—and by extension, her messy, rebellious lifestyle—to a "maiden aunt" based on Marianne Moore. As noted earlier, Moore had upset Plath by calling her poems "bitter" and "averse." Now Plath was striking back. "I am bitter? I'm averse?" the speaker proclaims, after warning her visitor against getting too close to her appliances (the frost-box makes "Millions of needly glass cakes!" and the furnace burns the speaker's hair off). Plath, a model hausfrau, uses the metaphor of the clean house to mock oppressive feminine standards of soul-deadening propriety. The speaker's house is "a bit of a mess!" and she meets her visitor in "slippers and housedress with no lipstick!" The exclamation points emphasize an extremity of emotion that might just be unseemly. Plath's speaker doesn't care whether she makes the correct impression on this conservative dowager.

"The Tour" is Plath's message to Moore, whose persona and work she angrily mocks as chilly, oppressive, and life-denying. (The fact that Moore had asked Hughes to omit certain poems that used sexual language from *The Hawk in the Rain* only fueled Plath's indignation.) "The Tour" was written about three months before the publication of *The Feminine Mystique*, but it expresses a similar exhaustion with—and rebellion from—traditional mores of femininity. It also espouses a rawer, more taboo aesthetic that both Plath and Hughes, as well as Lowell, Sexton, and Alvarez, had embraced. In this sense, "The Tour" itself stands as a fitting example of the Nietzschean brand of philosophy that animates *Ariel*: these poems would embrace freedom of expression and disavow puritanism. They would refuse to submit or please. Plath knew their impact would be shocking and revolutionary, as she hints in "The Tour" when the speaker tells her visitor to "Toddle on home to tea now in your flat hat" while she enjoys "Lemon tea and earwig biscuits—creepy-creepy. | You'd not want that." By highlighting her speaker's "weirdnesses," Plath diminishes Moore's aesthetic and emboldens her own. Plath here throws down the gauntlet; nothing less than the direction of modern poetry is at stake.

This unapologetic boldness animates much of *Ariel*. Plath began on October 1 with "The Detective" and "The Courage of Shutting Up"; both portray female speakers as survivors of violence. In the latter poem, a tongue in danger of being "cut out" is finally unleashed to speak the truth: "it is dangerous." Plath's poems, likewise, will perform this "dangerous" unleashing as Plath herself refuses to remain silent in the wake of her husband's betrayal. Plath's speakers in *Ariel* will blast sentimental feminine ideas. They have nothing left to lose, and everything to gain, from speaking their truths. Hughes's leave-taking was the catalyst for this new tone, which had first announced itself with "Zoo Keeper's Wife," but the themes of rebirth, resurrection, transcendence, motherhood, and depression had been part of Plath's oeuvre for years. Now, a more determined rebelliousness and a more flagrant disregard for propriety propelled the poems aloft. Plath would no longer "shut up." The poems of *Ariel* insist upon being heard, foreshadowing the critic Maggie Nelson's later sense that "the injunction to behave appropriately...is but a death knell for art-making, especially for women."

Plath referred to the next group of poems she wrote that October as "the Bee sequence" in her letters. "The Bee Meeting," "The Arrival of the Bee Box," "Stings," "The Swarm," and "Wintering" were based upon her experience of beekeeping in Devon during the summer of 1962, and they also drew upon the legacy of her father Otto Plath, whose magnum opus was his academic study *Bumblebees and Their Ways*. Plath's bee poems speak of power and powerlessness, vulnerability and strength. "Stings" and "Wintering" are the most personal of the sequence; in "Stings" the speaker compares herself to the queen bees in her hives:

> I am no drudge
> Though for years I have eaten dust
> And dried plates with my dense hair.

She has seen her "strangeness evaporate, | Blue dew from dangerous skin." No longer will she accept subordination: "I | Have a self to recover, a queen." She will have her revenge on the feminine domestic:

> Now she is flying
> More terrible than she ever was, red
> Scar in the sky, red comet
> Over the engine that killed her—
> The mausoleum, the wax house.

Here Plath implies that "the engine that killed her" is the house itself, which had become a "mausoleum." In "Wintering," the last poem in Plath's original ordering of *Ariel*, the speaker ponders the bees she keeps in her cellar. "They have got rid of the men," Plath writes. The speaker wonders, "Will the hive survive . . . ?" and asserts, at the poem's end, "The bees are flying. They taste the spring." Plath wanted her book to end hopefully with the word spring, an enduring poetic theme since childhood.

In the wake of Hughes's departure from Court Green, Plath wrote "The Applicant," which presents marriage as a con sold to unwitting young brides and grooms. The portrait of the bride is particularly brutal. Plath again takes aim at the feminine domestic: "It can sew, it can cook, || It can talk, talk, talk." On the following day, October 12, Plath wrote several drafts of "Daddy," her most famous and controversial poem. Plath writes in nursery rhyme cadences which belie the poem's sophistication and literary antecedents: "You do not do, you do not do | Any more, black shoe," the poem begins. Plath's speaker conjures her father, whom she compares to a Nazi, and imagines herself a Jew sent to a concentration camp. Though Plath has been heavily criticized for appropriating Holocaust imagery in "Daddy," she was under the impression that her maternal great-grandmother was Jewish or part-Jewish. Plath herself said of the poem's speaker, "Her case is complicated by the fact that her father was also a Nazi and her mother very possibly part Jewish. In the daughter the two strains marry and paralyze each other—she has to act out the awful little allegory once over before she is free of it." Plath also took aim at Hughes in the poem, the "man in black with a Meinkampf look || And a love of the rack and the screw. | And I said I do, I do." While the poem does not contain a regular rhyme scheme, it retains, like many *Ariel* poems, formal elements—the "ooh" sound provides an aural coherence from beginning to end, while the stanzas are all the same length. These formalist techniques act as barriers containing the poem's whirlwind of anger, while the poem's allusions to Eliot's "The Waste Land," Sexton's "My Friend, My Friend," and Hughes's "Out" belie its simplistic stutter—a stutter that suggests the bankruptcy of language itself in the wake of Holocaust. At the poem's end, the speaker seems to kill off the father, and perhaps, by extension, patriarchy itself: "Daddy, daddy, you bastard, I'm through." "Daddy" was embraced by feminism, despite the fact that (as we will see) it was condemned by prominent writers such as Helen Vendler, Irving Howe, Harold Bloom, and Seamus Heaney for what they considered its irresponsible use of Holocaust imagery. Yet Plath's use of surrealism was innovative, as was the bereaved daughter's expression of anger and hurt. "Daddy" helped introduce female anger into the poetic lexicon, and open up new parameters for the elegy.

"The Jailer," which followed "Daddy," features a woman who is "drugged and raped" and kept captive by a male Bluebeard. The speaker is brutalized ("Hung, starved, burned, hooked") and emotionally suffocated: "being free" is an "impossibility." But the company of women is almost as oppressive in "Lesbos," which takes aim at domesticity and female friendship. Plath locates domesticity's heart in the kitchen of a friend, where the speaker senses "Viciousness" and is nauseated by the "stink of fat and baby crap." "The smog of cooking" is "the smog of hell." The speaker leaves the erstwhile friend's home stewing with hate, "Thick, thick."

"Fever 103°," which Plath finished on October 20, was inspired by a high fever she had recently experienced. Instead of condemning feminine symbols and archetypes, as she had in "Lesbos," Plath now interrogates them. She begins almost philosophically: "Pure? What does it mean?"—aware of the myriad ways the answer has shaped women's lives. Plath plays with the trope of purity through the ages—particularly men's demand for it—as the speaker hallucinates and imagines herself a virgin whose sullied "selves" ("old whore petticoats") dissolve while she ascends to Paradise. Plath treats the symbols of "pure" femininity with a deflating irony as the speaker imagines herself surrounded by roses, kisses, and cherubim, "By whatever these pink things mean." As in "The Tour" and "Lesbos," Plath mocks the trappings of female propriety and sentimentality—though here, the send-up is more exuberant. Yet even as Plath mocks the idea of purity, the speaker's longing for it gives the poem an ambiguous edge.

The speaker in "Lady Lazarus," on the other hand, revels in bodily corruption. Lady Lazarus has come back from the dead before: "Dying | Is an art, like everything else. | I do it exceptionally well." She now taunts her audience, the "peanut-crunching crowd," who has paid to see her die again. Plath uses grotesque imagery—maggots, eye pits, "sour breath"—to parody the "big strip tease" Lady Lazarus performs under this surreal big-top. Lady Lazarus's face is "Bright as a Nazi lampshade." Later in the poem, she dissolves into a "cake of soap, | A wedding ring, | A gold filling." Plath's seemingly blithe use of these images for their shock-value angered critics, and is still controversial. But the poem ought not to be dismissed. Its sophisticated use of irony and performance turns the mirror back upon the reader: Plath asks *us* to question our own attraction to extremities of death and destruction. After all, an audience has paid handsomely to see this living corpse and Nazi victim perform her "big strip tease." Plath's message may be closer to that of Susan Sontag, who famously questioned the morality of viewing Holocaust photographs. That Lady Lazarus is presented as a victim of fascism is no accident: Plath here makes a connection between fascism, itself an extreme form of masculine violence, and the spectacle of violence against women. Plath wrote most of "Lady Lazarus" during the most intense period of the Cuban Missile Crisis, October 22 to October 27, 1962, which may explain the anger toward men (Herr Doktor, Herr Enemy) who were once again steering the world toward apocalypse less than two decades after the Second World War.

"Lady Lazarus" treats the confessional impulse, too, with deep irony and cynicism. Plath's invocation of the strip tease trope invokes pornography, but it is not physical arousal the audience has paid for—rather, Plath suggests, it is the equally satisfying spectacle of watching a woman fall apart. Plath understood that a woman's fall from grace was a form of misogynist entertainment as old as time. Both Plath, as she writes, and Lady Lazarus, as she performs, are aware of this sexist dynamic, which is perhaps why Lady Lazarus promises at the poem's end to "rise" like a Phoenix out of the ash and "eat men like air"—a line that seems to pun on the idea of an empty threat. The revenge fantasy is just that; Plath draws attention to women's powerlessness in the face of brute masculine violence epitomized by fascism. Like "Edge," "Lady Lazarus" satirizes the idea that a dead woman is "perfected," and gives the impression of having been written posthumously. It is as if Plath foresaw her own literary legacy as a confessional poet, and predicts her readers' voracious appetite for the most sensational, death-ridden details from her life.

"Purdah," written during the same week as "Lady Lazarus," reframes the story of Clytemnestra's murder of Agamemnon from Clytemnestra's point of view. "Purdah" seemingly picks up where "Lady Lazarus" leaves off, with the promise to destroy men. The end of "Purdah" conjures the famous murder: "The shriek in the bath." Plath's largely sympathetic portrayals of traditionally reviled Classical heroines such as Clytemnestra and Medea were innovative. In her poems, they are given the chance to explain, if not justify, their acts of vengeance against the men who had betrayed them. They are no longer silenced.

Plath wrote "Ariel," which she eventually chose for the title of her collection, on her 30th birthday. This celebratory poem invokes creative transcendence and rebirth. Ariel was the name of the horse Plath rode during her riding lessons in Devon during the fall of 1962; in the poem the speaker imagines herself on an early morning horseback ride. The ride is fast, and liberating: Plath invokes Lady Godiva's naked ride through Coventry, protesting her husband's mistreatment of her, as she ascends imaginary hills and dales. Plath told others that during this time she got up at 4:00 a.m. to write poems before her children awoke. In "Ariel," riding becomes a metaphor for writing (there is even an aural pun), an activity in which the speaker loses herself and which gives her nearly as much pleasure as orgasm—"And now I | Foam to wheat, a glitter of seas." But suddenly the spell is broken: the "child's cry" in the next room "Melts in the wall." The speaker ignores it, imagining herself "the arrow" flying "Suicidal" toward transcendence—becoming her art just as Yeats imagines in "Sailing to Byzantium."

In *The Bell Jar*, Esther Greenwood mocks Mrs. Willard's bromide that men are the arrows and women are the places the arrow "shoots off from." On her 30th birthday, Plath was revisiting this idea; its blatant sexism had always bothered her. Now, she was rewriting this tired script: in "Ariel," the woman is the arrow. This is the kind of femininity that Plath can get behind—strong, surefooted, rebellious, independent; one that embraces children but disavows maternal martyrdom and even men themselves. (It was around this time that Plath wrote to Bill Merwin that she didn't want to be anyone's wife.) "Ariel" may have been Plath's resolution to herself on the cusp of a new, independent chapter in her own life. The dashes and exclamation points throughout the poem propel its momentum. And as in "Daddy" and "Lady Lazarus," Plath adheres to three-lined stanzas with an irregular but patterned rhyme scheme that keeps "Ariel" from flying off the page. Plath's use of a racial slur in the fourth stanza, however, has mired this poem in contemporary controversy, and resulted in more critical attention to Plath and race.

The same day Plath finished "Ariel," she also wrote the short, exquisite "Poppies in October," which surrealistically marries beauty with existential dread. Like "Ariel," the poem begins in the morning, but now there are harbingers of destruction: a woman in an ambulance; carbon monoxide in the atmosphere;

suspicious, dull eyes under bowler hats. The backdrop of the Cuban Missile Crisis suggests that the specter of nuclear annihilation was not far from Plath's imagination, and may help explain the poem's dystopian sensibility. The same is true of her late October poem "Nick and the Candlestick." There, Plath describes a baby's nursery—again, surrealistically—as an underground cave, dripping with stalactites and inhabited by "Black bat airs" and "Cold homicides." Whether these shadowy ills reflect the mindscape of depression, apocalyptic apprehension, or something else is unclear, though as Paul Giles has noted, Plath's reference to "mercuric | Atoms that cripple" and poison wells suggests nuclear fallout, as does the underground shelter. The mother tries to ward these horrors off: "Love, love, | I have hung our cave with roses, | With soft rugs— || The last of Victoriana." The child is the final remaining symbol of rightness, "the one | Solid" in a world on the brink of annihilation. The Irish poet Eavan Boland felt that in this poem, and in "By Candlelight," Plath was revising the male Romantic definition of the sublime. Plath, Boland says, gave women poets confidence that "Standing in a room in the winter half-light before the wonder of a new child is aesthetics."

Even when writing about "ugly" subjects, Plath never abandoned poetic form. Her use of rhyme and regular tercets in "Fever 103°," "Lyonnesse," "Amnesiac," "Ariel," "Poppies in October," "Nick and the Candlestick," "Purdah," and "Lady Lazarus" keep them firmly grounded in the tradition of lyric poetry. "Daddy" and other poems from this period also have regular stanza lengths. But these poems were still too shocking to editors like Howard Moss at *The New Yorker*, who rejected nearly every poem Plath sent to him in October, November, and December of 1962. Plath thought that these new poems were her best yet, and felt she had finally succeeded once and for all in breaking out of her "glass caul." But the stream of rejection letters that arrived from New York that fall suggested otherwise.

London on her own

Plath planned to spend the winter of 1962–3 in the west of Ireland with her children, far from Hughes. But she soon changed her mind after three visits to London that fall, and decided to look for a flat in the city, where she would be closer to bookstores, art galleries, and the theater, as well as supportive friends like Alvarez, for whom she had developed romantic feelings. She was thrilled when, during one of these trips to London, she came across a three-bedroom, two-story flat for rent in a townhouse around the corner from her old flat at Chalcot Square. There was a blue plaque on the house noting that Yeats had once lived there. For Plath, this was a sign that her decision to move to London instead of Ireland was the right one: "my work should be blessed," she wrote her mother. Plath eventually put up a year's rent, with financial help from her American family, to secure the flat. Giddy with hope, she prepared for a new life (Figure 9).

Plath moved to 23 Fitzroy Rd. on December 9, 1962, with her children. She immediately began pursuing leads for an au pair. Hughes came to see the children on weekends, visits that were emotionally draining for Plath. The couple still planned to divorce. Not long after she moved into the new flat, she learned that her American publisher Knopf had rejected *The Bell Jar*. Plath had always cared a great deal about American publication, and she took this rejection very hard. A potential romantic relationship with Alvarez fizzled out around Christmas, and Plath and the children were again ill with respiratory ailments. In January 1963, she chronicled her difficulties in a short piece, "Snow Blitz," about her experience during the coldest British winter in a century. Her pipes froze and her electricity and heat were intermittent. Stuck in a cold flat in bad weather with sick children and ill herself, Plath's depression, which had resurfaced after Hughes's affair, worsened.

The Bell Jar was officially released by Heinemann on January 14 and received good reviews—some excellent—in the British press.

9. Yeats's House, 23 Fitzroy Road, London.

But, according to Hughes, Plath was disappointed that the coverage was not more laudatory. She had hoped *The Bell Jar* would become a bestseller that would help her fund her new life, for she did not want to depend on Hughes's monthly alimony and child support. But the novel did not catch fire, and during the third week of January she learned it had been rejected by Hughes's

American publisher, Harper & Row. Plath was increasingly despondent, and her mental health deteriorated. Most friends and neighbors who visited her that January and early February found her gaunt and melancholy, the children sickly—though she reassured friends and family in her letters home that she was in good hands with her doctor and was receiving treatment for her "flu." None had any idea how deeply depression had taken hold. Hughes remembered coming for sherry to celebrate the publication of *The Bell Jar* with her that January, and they sometimes spoke of reconciling.

A bright spot during this grim period was Plath's broadcast review of Donald Hall's *Penguin Anthology of Contemporary American Poetry* for the BBC. (The anthology did not include her own work.) In her review, she spoke of the "surrealist" tendencies of modern American poets, as well as the role played by the "analyst's couch." Plath hinted at her admiration for the new confessional aesthetic. Speaking of Robert Lowell's poetry, she wrote of "The flashing elaborate carapace of *Lord Weary's Castle* dropped for *Life Studies*, walking the tightrope of the psyche naked." She noted the "inwardness" and "plummeting subjectivity" of Lowell's images.

By this time, she had found an au pair and had begun writing again. But the tone of these new poems differed from those she had written earlier that fall. The sense of propulsion, exaltation, and rage that had driven those verses had stalled. Now, the lyric self was pensive, apprehensive, overshadowed. Between January 28 and February 5, according to Hughes, Plath wrote or revised 12 poems. The first of this group was "Sheep in Fog," a draft of which she had already written in December. Now she revised the poem, stripping it of earlier references to the Phaeton and Helios myth so all that remained was a stark landscape that reveals itself, over the course of the poem, as a mindscape of depression. At the poem's end, the speaker, riding atop her "slow" horse, ponders the "far | Fields" that "threaten | To let me through to a heaven | Starless and fatherless, a dark water." The gentle assonance in these lines—the soft "a" and "e" sounds—are a kind of siren song tempting the speaker ever closer to a psychic abyss.

Other strong poems from this late period include "Kindness," finished on February 1, which, like the October poems "The Tour" and "Lesbos," takes aim at feminine propriety. "Dame Kindness," possibly inspired by Plath's mother, offers tea and sympathy, but the speaker balks: "The blood jet is poetry, | There is no stopping it." The poem's famous ending suggests the dramatic transformation that Plath herself underwent after Hughes's departure while writing *Ariel*. In "Words," also finished on February 1, the speaker expresses doubt about the lasting significance of her art, and its ability to retain meaning: "Years later I | Encounter them on the road— || Words dry and riderless..." The poem suggests failure; the "riderless" words have escaped the poet's control. In "Ariel," the horse was Pegasus, and the ride itself a metaphor for poetic inspiration. Now, in "Sheep in Fog" and "Words," the ride has slowed. Plath's speakers are burdened by loss, insignificance, doubt, despair, and, finally, a deadly paralysis ("fixed stars | Govern a life").

Plath wrote her last two surviving poems, "Balloons" and "Edge," on February 5. Though the poems appear to have quite different themes, both address forces the speaker cannot control. In "Balloons," Plath's speaker describes her delight as she watches her children play with balloons, which, in their literal lightness, function as a metaphor for innocence. The tone of the poem quickly shifts, however, when the little boy accidentally pops one. He falls back on his bottom, stunned, left to contemplate "A red | Shred in his little fist." The sudden, violent explosion, though benign, disrupts the poem's light tone. The boy's confused reaction speaks to breakage and loss of innocence—the earliest of many expulsions from the garden. Plath takes an otherwise comical domestic moment and invests it with dread and foreboding; the rhyme of "red" and "shred" suggest wreckage. The boy's mother seems to understand that what the poet Eavan Boland called the "long fall from grace" has begun, and she is powerless to stop it.

"Edge," like "Balloons," is another poem about mothers and children. But this time, the familial portrait is dark. A mother-speaker lies dead with her two children in what the critic Judith Kroll has called a "frozen and eternal tableau." The poem's famous first lines read, "The woman is perfected. | Her dead || Body wears the smile of accomplishment." The woman wears a toga, her feet bare, with her dead children at her breast while an impassive moon hangs in the sky. The Medea-like speaker has "folded" her children "back into her body" like a rose that closes nightly in a garden. The allusion to the pastoral harkens back to Plath's childhood and adolescent poems about the redemptive power of spring—a leitmotif in her poetry up until the very end of her life. Indeed, in an influential, sympathetic reading of "Edge," the critic Helen Vendler interpreted the mother's murder of her children as a "protective" effort to save them from the world's horrors.

Still, the poem has often been interpreted as a kind of posthumous suicide note that pushes the confessional genre to the extreme. And yet this poem is intensely *literary*: it alludes to Shakespeare's *Antony and Cleopatra*, the poetry of W. B. Yeats ("He Wishes His Beloved Were Dead"), Sara Teasdale ("I Shall Not Care"), Robert Graves, and D. H. Lawrence. It also draws upon the surrealist art of Giorgio de Chirico, the Italian painter whose work had inspired Plath's earlier poem "The Disquieting Muses." De Chirico had created paintings of women in togas lying down on slabs near arched buildings that cast long shadows as trains move in the distance. Plath had seen one of these paintings, *Ariadne*, at the Metropolitan Museum of Art in New York City in 1958, and had written an earlier, adolescent poem "To Ariadne (deserted by Theseus)." Plath often used the word "deserted" in her letters to others about Hughes. Now she was revisiting this theme again, speaking through two deserted Classical heroines, Medea and Ariadne, giving them a voice. Though Vendler situates "Edge" within a life-affirming pastoral tradition, there is no denying the poem's bleakness, horror, and resignation, embodied by the indifferent moon who stares down, sinister and regal, "from her hood of bone." Plath ends, icily, "She is used to this sort of thing. | Her blacks crackle and drag."

The same week Plath wrote "Balloons" and "Edge" in early February, she wrote her last letters to her mother, Dr. Beuscher, and a few close friends. She told them she was feeling "grim." She was seeing a sympathetic local doctor who had put her on an anti-depressant and was trying to arrange a bed for her in a psychiatric facility during what would be the last week of her life. Plath admitted her loneliness and despair in her last letter to Dr. Beuscher, in which she candidly revealed her fear that she was falling into another severe depression that would lead to institutionalization or suicide: "What appals me is the return of my madness, my paralysis, my fear & vision of the worst—cowardly withdrawal, a mental hospital, lobotomies. . . . I am scared to death I shall just pull up the psychic shroud & give up." She knew her poems were "very good but, I feel written on the edge of madness."

A week later, on February 11, Plath died by self-inflicted carbon monoxide poisoning from her gas oven as her children slept upstairs. She had opened their windows so the gas would not affect them, and left milk and bread for them in their room. They were rescued by a visiting nurse who had been scheduled to arrive that morning, and a workman who had let the nurse into the flat.

Plath was buried in West Yorkshire on a high hillside cemetery in the village of Heptonstall, down the road from Hughes's parents' home. A small number of mourners attended; few of Plath's friends from London or Devon came because of the difficulty of traveling up to Yorkshire in winter. Today thousands of visitors leave pens on her grave each year.

Chapter 6
Afterlives

Posthumous reception

Plath's August 1953 disappearance made headlines all over America, but her suicide 10 years later barely merited a mention in any newspaper. There was a perfunctory news story in the *St Pancras Chronicle*, buried far from the front page. Gas poisoning was a common method of suicide, particularly for women, and the article gave the impression that Plath's death would not have been reported if not for her marriage to Hughes: it described the "tragic death" of a "30-year-old authoress Mrs. Sylvia Plath Hughes, wife of one of Britain's best known modern poets, Ted Hughes."

It was Alvarez who helped bring attention to Plath's death and brilliant career, on her own terms, in an article dated February 17 in the *Observer*. Titled "A Poet's Epitaph," it featured a story about Plath, her revolutionary work, and her death. It was an obituary of sorts, but a cryptic one; Alvarez wrote that she "died suddenly" at age 30. The article was accompanied by a photograph of Plath and her infant, and four poems, "The Fearful," "Kindness," "Contusion," and "Edge." Alvarez helped shape Plath's early reception, which called attention to her brilliance, but he also initiated the myth of Plath as an oracular priestess. He wrote that in her final months she had been "writing continuously almost as though possessed." Still, he gave Plath her due. He called her a "genius," and claimed her recent poetry "represents a totally new breakthrough in modern verse, and establishes her, I think, as the most gifted woman poet of our time.... The loss to literature is inestimable."

Because Plath and Hughes were still married at the time of her death, Hughes inherited her literary estate; he now controlled her work and literary legacy. But Hughes was shell-shocked and overwhelmed with practical responsibilities in the weeks following Plath's death. Plath's brother Warren and his wife Margaret wanted to raise Frieda and Nicholas in America, but Hughes, after some consideration, decided against this course of action. A well-meaning friend also offered to take Nicholas, who was almost 13 months old at the time of Plath's death, but Hughes could not part with his son. He was in a fog of grief, and he blamed himself for Plath's suicide in letters to others. But he felt an obligation to promote Plath's work, and began sending out Plath's poems shortly after her death. He hoped his efforts would secure Plath's legacy and provide a financial cushion for her children.

Hughes's endorsement was powerful, as was Alvarez's; editors who had previously rejected Plath's work were suddenly eager to accept her poems. Plath had secured acceptances from *The Atlantic* and *The London Magazine* before her death, so some of these poems were due to be published anyway. But her sudden and tragic suicide likely accelerated her unpublished poems' reach and draw. *The New Yorker*, which had rejected Plath's poems throughout the fall of 1962, published seven of them in its August 1963 issue. Ten appeared in the 1963 October issue of *Encounter*. Major poets, and the reading public, started to take note. In October of that year, Robert Lowell wrote to Elizabeth Bishop:

Have you read the posthumous poems by Sylvia Plath?
A terrifying and stunning group has come out in the last Encounter.
You probably know the story of her suicide. The poems are all

about it. They seem as good to me as Emily Dickinson at the moment. Of course they are as extreme as one can bear, rather more so, but whatever wrecked her life somehow gave an edge, freedom and even control, to her poetry. There's a lot of surrealism which relieves the heat of direct memory, touches me, and I'm pretty sure touches your quiet humor. She is far better certainly than Sexton . . . and almost makes one feel at first reading that almost all other poetry is about nothing. Still, it's searingly extreme, a triumph by a hair, that one almost wished had never come about.

Hughes arranged for *Ariel* to be published by Faber and Faber in 1965, albeit in a different order than the one Plath had originally arranged. He also excluded several poems that Plath had included in her original manuscript, including "The Rabbit Catcher," though he retained the two poems that would become the most controversial in the collection, "Daddy" and "Lady Lazarus." Hughes took the liberty of adding 13 1962–3 poems that Plath had not included in her original *Ariel*, among them "Sheep in Fog," "Words," "Kindness," and "Edge." He felt he was making *Ariel* a better book by including these masterful late poems, but his rearrangement of Plath's manuscript infuriated feminist critics. Perhaps most disturbingly, Hughes's rearrangement of *Ariel* also gave the impression that Plath was on a course for suicide. She had begun her version of *Ariel* with the poem "Morning Song" and the word "Love," and ended it with the poem "Wintering" and word "spring," invoking the theme of resurrection which had interested her since childhood. These literary choices suggested her own imminent rebirth. Hughes erased this more hopeful trajectory when he ended his version of *Ariel* with the considerably darker poems "Contusion," "Edge," and "Words." Plath and Hughes's daughter Frieda later reissued *Ariel*, in the original order Plath had intended, in 2004.

But the reading public knew nothing about Plath's original order of *Ariel* when it was published in 1965. It sold 15,000 copies in its first month of publication—an extremely high number for a poetry collection. Hughes gave permission to Faber and Faber to publish *The Bell Jar* under Plath's own name in 1966; in 1971, it was published in America by Harper & Row, who had rejected it in early 1963. The novel became a bestseller, just as Plath had hoped, selling over three million copies to date and becoming a cultural reference point.

During the 1970s, when the women's movement began to embrace Plath, Hughes commented bitterly that she had become its "Patron Saint," a role he did not think she would have accepted. He always felt she was "'Laurentian,' not 'women's lib'"—that she and her work espoused sexual freedom in the face of puritanism, rather than the pursuit of women's equality. He thought Plath would have had the same attitude toward feminism as his friend Doris Lessing, whose novel *The Golden Notebook* had been hailed as a feminist masterpiece but who spurned the feminist label. Hughes's feelings on this matter, and his rearrangement of *Ariel*, put him on a collision course with the women's movement, and a symbolic custody battle ensued. As Plath's reputation within the movement ascended, Hughes became a target of feminist rage. In the early 1970s, the poet Robin Morgan accused him of murdering Sylvia Plath in her poem "The Arraignment," which outraged him and his friends. He soon stopped giving readings in America, which he called "enemy country." He felt besieged, swept up in a movement that demanded a villain in Plath's story. The rancor on both sides increased, and the Plath Estate often refused feminist scholars permission to quote Plath's work. Plath's grave in Heptonstall, which read "Sylvia Plath Hughes," was defaced several times; under cover of darkness, people chiseled "Hughes" off the stone, prompting a public debate between Hughes and feminist scholars in the pages of *The Independent* and *The Guardian* in 1989 (Figure 10).

Plath's mother Aurelia had blamed Hughes for Plath's death in the immediate aftermath of Plath's suicide, as did Hughes himself; he expressed much guilt in letters to others in the weeks and

IN MEMORY
SYLVIA PLATH HUGHES
1932 — 1963
EVEN AMIDST FIERCE FLAMES
THE GOLDEN LOTUS CAN BE PLANTED

10. Sylvia Plath's grave, Heptonstall, West Yorkshire.

months following Plath's death. Though Aurelia's feelings toward
Hughes softened somewhat over the years, she was upset that she
no longer owned the letters, drawings, and other ephemera her
daughter had sent to her since childhood. All of this was now,
technically, Hughes's property because Plath had died intestate.
Hughes became more sympathetic toward Aurelia as emotions

cooled and both found themselves blamed for Plath's suicide. In the 1970s he allowed Aurelia to assemble a collection of Plath's letters to her, which she titled *Letters Home*. But this project, too, became mired in controversy. *Letters Home* was a curated selection of mainly cheerful letters that gave the impression Plath had rarely, if ever, suffered from physical or mental illness. Hughes had also asked Aurelia to remove Plath's nastier comments about friends who were still alive, and forbade her from publishing damning accounts of his own behavior. Aurelia had wanted to show the world Plath's life-loving side; the book was supposed to be a counterpoint to Esther Greenwood's depressed character, often identified with Plath, in *The Bell Jar*. But the effort backfired: *Letters Home* elicited charges of censorship and whitewashing when it was published. A similar critical reception awaited the abridged version of Plath's *Journals*, which was selected by Hughes and edited by Francis McCullough. Again, many of the more distraught or subversive entries were left out. Hughes himself had admitted to burning Plath's last journal so that her children would never have to read her final, searing entries, though he also hinted obliquely that the journal might still exist. It is possible that Plath's last, lost novel, *Double Exposure*—unfinished at the time of her death—may also resurface someday.

P(l)athography

Male poets have long been regarded as secular prophets touched by fire. But women poets who try to claim this lofty mantle often find their attempts likened to witchcraft or other quasi-occult practices by the male critical establishment. Plath understood this, and played with the idea of black magic in her poetry. Her ironic command of this trope is clear in "Daddy" and "Lady Lazarus," while Anne Sexton famously compared her speaker to a witch in her best-known poem, "Her Kind." (Sexton writes, "I have gone out, a possessed witch, | haunting the black air, braver at night," and concludes, "A woman like that is not a woman, quite. | I have been her kind.") But Alvarez's labeling of Plath as "a priestess emptied out by the rites of her cult" had unfortunate ramifications for Plath's legacy. Plath had been intrigued by the figure of the Egyptian goddess Isis, and both she and Hughes were fascinated by Robert Graves's book *The White Goddess*. Still, the posthumous identification of Plath with priestly rites, possession, and witchcraft is at worst sexist and at best patronizing. Plath herself wrote to her friend Mel Woody in 1954, "I am a damn good high priestess of the intellect." Well before *Ariel*, Plath was already playing with the stereotypical trope of the woman poet, and making clear ("of the intellect") that she meant to redefine it. The identification of Plath as priestess was so strong that it even affected Plath's largely female readership, which would come to be represented in the media, and by Hughes himself, as a "cult." This reductive and sexist label has had a pernicious staying power; the term is still used blithely in reviews and newspaper articles as shorthand for Plath's readers. Plath cherished what she called her "weirdnesses," but she is no more a witch than a saint. The bogus characterization of her as a "priestess," along with her story of depression and suicide, stalled biographical attempts to consider her, in Hermione Lee's words, "a professional writer first."

In the years after her death, Plath became a cipher. Although Plath's life makes a tempting case study for psychoanalytically minded biographers and literary critics—as we have seen, *The Bell Jar* was based on Plath's own breakdown, suicide attempt, and recovery at McLean Hospital, while she drew upon her own psychodrama in poems like "Daddy" and "The Colossus"—Plath blurred the borders between her life and her work in innovative ways that complicate her biographers' task. Plath's status as a confessional poet who seems to tell all in her fiction and poetry also blurs those borders. Early biographies framed Plath as primarily the subject of her art, rather than its creator. By 1993, when Janet Malcolm published *The Silent Woman: Sylvia Plath and Ted Hughes*, the landscape of Plath biography—or so Malcolm intimated—was littered with unfinished manuscripts and nervous breakdowns. This situation was partly a result of practical difficulties of working with the Plath Estate, which was effectively controlled by Hughes's sister Olwyn. Both Hugheses had little regard for most Plath biographers, particularly Edward Butscher, Ronald Hayman, and Paul Alexander. Butscher famously pathologized Plath in his 1976 biography, calling Plath neurotic and schizophrenic and sexually confused over the death of her father; Hayman (1991) and Alexander (1991) both began their biographies with Plath's death, giving the impression that hers was a life set on a course for suicide. Linda Wagner-Martin's feminist biography of Plath (1987) was well received, but short on detail and marred, at times, by armchair psychoanalysis (e.g., "The sense of dependence and the narcissism that were to mark, and sometimes ruin, Sylvia's relationships in the future clearly originated in her childhood fear of abandonment").

The Plath Estate refused to cooperate with any of these biographers. Ted and Olwyn Hughes did, however, invite Lois Ames and, eventually, Harriet Rosenstein to write Plath's biography in the 1970s (neither of them finished the task), and supported Judith Kroll's Gravesian scholarly study of Plath, *Chapters in a Mythology*. The poet Anne Stevenson was given full permission to quote Plath's work in her biography, but over the years of research and writing, Stevenson lost authorial control of the book to Olwyn, who had disliked Plath when she was alive and who insisted Stevenson portray her in a harsh light. The result was a famously negative and controversial biography of Plath, *Bitter Fame*, published in 1989. Stevenson suggested that Plath's desire to write was pathological, and that Plath's "gift was for romantic self-aggrandizing ... Sylvia was trapped in her story, condemned to telling it again and again to whoever would listen. She was indeed cursed." Stevenson also emphasized the melodramatic idea that Plath wrote to stave off her demons: "Haunted by a fear of her own disintegration, she kept herself together by defining herself, writing constantly about herself, so that everyone could see her there, fighting and conquering an outside world that forever threatened her frail being." Malcolm, in *The Silent Woman*, focused much of her discussion on the troubled composition and legacy of *Bitter Fame*, though she also wrote negative commentaries about Butscher and Alexander's biographies. For Malcolm, Plath biography itself provided the necessary evidence that biography as a genre was ethically dubious, if not downright abusive. She famously compared biographers to burglars rifling through drawers of private possessions.

The Silent Woman had a chilling effect on Plath biography. Over 20 years passed between Alexander's 1991 biography *Rough Magic* and Carl Rollyson's *American Isis* (2013) and Andrew Wilson's *Mad Girl's Love Song: Sylvia Plath and Life Before Ted* (2013). Both of these books received mixed reviews; their titles suggest that the myth of Plath as priestess was still as popular as ever 50 years after her death. Wilson's book, in particular, painted Plath's ambition and determination to become a great writer as pathological: he wrote that she was "addicted to achievement in the same way an alcoholic is hooked on booze," while her "competitive drive" was "pathological" and stemmed from "interior hollowness." The Pulitzer Prize-winning biographer Caroline Fraser has commented upon the biographical double standard in which ambitious men are praised, while ambitious women are pathologized. Fraser says, "Writing about women who have achieved a modicum of influence can often feel like watching someone on a precipice: One foot wrong, and it's the block, the pillory, or the head in the oven." That Plath's suicide has become a crude shorthand for the limits of female ambition is not surprising. Plath herself links Esther's electroshock treatment, in *The Bell Jar*, to existential punishment: after one of her early treatments, Esther says, "I wondered what terrible thing it was I had done." Her thoughts suggest the veracity of Fraser's claim that "Power and ambition in women are often hidden, buried, shrouded, veiled, disguised, crushed, thwarted, mocked, diminished, warped, punished, or excoriated. Women oriented toward ambition may have concealed such a desire even from themselves."

In 2020, I published a 1,117-page biography, *Red Comet: The Short Life and Blazing Art of Sylvia Plath*, which focused on Plath's struggle to become a great writer. This was the story I wanted to tell because it was so clearly the one Plath tells about herself in her surviving journals and letters. *Red Comet*, whose title comes from Plath's poem "Stings," was the first biography—though surely not the last—to benefit from a wealth of new material, including all of Plath's surviving letters, newly opened archival collections, and new information about Plath's medical treatment. But there is no such thing as a definitive biography. New material will surface, ideological winds will shift, and new questions will emerge about Plath's life and times in the years to come.

Controversy and legacy

While Plath's work was being celebrated by feminist scholars such as Marjorie Perloff, Sandra Gilbert, Susan Gubar, Susan Van Dyne, Lynda Bundtzen, and many others, several important figures in the male critical establishment were attempting to remove her from the canon altogether. George Steiner framed this debate in 1965 when, reviewing *Ariel*, he called "Daddy" "one of the very few poems I know of in any language to come near the last horror. . . . It is the 'Guernica' of modern poetry." (The comparison likely would have pleased Plath, who had a reproduction of *Guernica* hanging in her Wellesley bedroom.) Yet Steiner worried Plath had committed "a subtle larceny" by appropriating the imagery of Auschwitz for her "own private design." Irving Howe and Harold Bloom both wrote scathing essays in the years that followed about what they considered Plath's irresponsible and offensive use of Holocaust imagery in some of her *Ariel* poems. Howe called Plath's use of such imagery "monstrous"; Bloom, "gratuitous and humanly offensive." Even Seamus Heaney, who admired Plath's work (Plath's "Lady Lazarus" may have influenced Heaney's portrayals of female bodies in his bog poems), agreed that "Daddy" was "so tangled up in biographical circumstances and rampages so permissively in the history of other people's sorrows that it simply withdraws its rights to our sympathy." Helen Vendler, who elsewhere celebrated Plath, felt that the poem's style was that of a "tantrum." Howe was unwilling to grant Plath any separation from her poetic speakers, and wrote that "Daddy" "persuades once again . . . how accurate T. S. Eliot was in saying 'The more perfect the artist, the more completely separate in him will be the man who suffers and the mind which creates.'" This was presumably the sort of statement that prompted the critic Jacqueline Rose to suggest that critics hostile to "confessional" poetry on aesthetic grounds were predisposed to find Plath's poetry both hysterical and immoral.

Historical circumstance helps explain Plath's use of these images in the early 1960s. At the time, she was very close to Al Alvarez, who was himself Jewish and had visited Auschwitz. He and Plath spoke of the concentration camps when she visited him in London in the fall of 1962. Alvarez, in *The New Poetry*, had suggested that English poets needed to face the horrors of the war and the bomb head-on, and that they had a duty, as artists, to bear witness to atrocity. English poetry, he complained, had become too "genteel," much as Robert Lowell had complained that American poetry at this time needed a "breakthrough" back to life. Plath may have felt that she was answering Alvarez's call to action by writing poems like "Daddy" and "Lady Lazarus." In a fall 1962 letter, Plath told her mother that no one wanted to hear that the "birdies still go tweet-tweet" after Belsen. The person who has suffered, "physical or psychological," Plath went on, wants "the full knowledge that somebody has been there & knows the worst." And, as several critics have noted, the Holocaust was a topical subject in the late 1950s and early 1960s. The film *The Diary of Anne Frank* was released in 1959; Elie Wiesel's *Night* in 1960. Adolf Eichmann was captured in Argentina in 1960, and his trial in Jerusalem from April to December 1961 was highly publicized. He was hanged in June 1962. As previously mentioned, Plath had been told by her mother—and she herself had told friends in England—that she had Jewish blood. Indeed, Plath herself spoke of the complexity of the speaker's dual Jewish–German identity in her BBC introduction to "Daddy."

But it was not just male writers who attacked Plath. Elizabeth Hardwick and Joyce Carol Oates read Plath's work through an unambiguously confessional lens and wrote influential essays about her art that trivialized Plath's agency as a writer and thinker. Hardwick interpreted "Edge" as extremist performance art: "When the curtain goes down," Hardwick wrote, "it is her own dead body there on the stage, sacrificed to her own plot." Oates evinced a similar frustration with Plath in her influential 1973 essay, "The Death Throes of Romanticism," in which she made little effort to separate Plath from her poem's speakers, and accused Plath of reveling in victimhood and spite in certain poems. Oates mentioned nothing about Plath's craft in her essay—that is, her masterful use of rhyme, meter, and overall formal technique. Oates used philosophical language but her point was blunt: she argued that Plath could not escape her separate, unhappy "self," an inability that led her to "dehumanize people" in her work. Such essays prompted a critical backlash, and major studies on Plath by Janet Badia, Judith Kroll, Tracy Brain, Steven Gould Axelrod, Robin Peel, Jacqueline Rose, Christina Britzolakis, Tim Kendall, Susan Van Dyne, Lynda Bundtzen, Gail Crowther, Peter K. Steinberg, myself, and others have called greater attention to Plath's irony and poetic technique.

Plath's reputation and popularity have survived these controversies, and have grown steadily in the years since her death. Her *Collected Poems*, which contains nearly all of her surviving post-1956 poems, was edited and introduced by Hughes and published in 1981. The book went on to win the Pulitzer Prize in Poetry—an achievement that would have delighted Plath, who submitted her work to scores of literary contests and who was disappointed not to have won the Yale Younger Poets Prize during her lifetime. Plath's unabridged journals, edited by Karen V. Kukil, were published in 2000, two years after Hughes's death and the publication of his poetic sequence about Plath, *Birthday Letters*. Editors Kukil and Peter K. Steinberg published all of Plath's known surviving letters in 2018 in a massive two-volume edition, a feat which helped advance Plath scholarship enormously. New scholarly editions of Plath's collected poems and collected prose are forthcoming.

Plath Studies, too, is flourishing. If feminism was the dominant lens through which Plath was viewed in the first two decades after her death, the scholarly dialogue has expanded to include Plath's relationship to confessionalism, formalism, transnationalism, the archive, the mid-century academy, literary networks, cultural studies, Ted Hughes, media studies, the environment, race, disability, and more. This breadth of approach and new directions in Plath scholarship suggest the continuing importance and relevance of her work decades after her death.

Plath also continues to command a large popular audience outside of the academy, and new books about Plath tend to generate media attention in major American and British newspapers and magazines. The Sylvia Plath Society was formed in 2019, and international conferences and online symposiums about Plath are plentiful. A new generation of readers continues to discover Plath through her work, which has found a massive online audience through Plath-related sites on Instagram, X, and Facebook. (There is even an X account with over 70,000 followers to date called Sylvia Plath's Food Diary, devoted to tweeting every meal Plath ever ate.) Plath's poems continue to stir controversy, but her legacy as one of the 20th century's most innovative, influential, and arresting poets is secure.

Further reading

Chapter 1: Icon and iconoclast

"the other Sylvia Plath": Tracy Brain, *The Other Sylvia Plath* (Routledge, 2001).

Jacqueline Rose, *The Haunting of Sylvia Plath* (Virago, 1991).

"second-wave feminism": For more on this movement, see Ruth Rosen, *The World Split Open: How the Modern Women's Movement Changed America* (Penguin, 2000).

"containment": See Deborah Nelson, *Pursuing Privacy in Cold War America* (Columbia University Press, 2002) and Elaine Tyler May, *Homeward Bound: American Families in the Cold War Era* (Basic Books, 1988; 2017).

"humble role of the housewife": Adlai Stevenson, "A Purpose for Modern Women," *Women's Home Companion* (September 1955), 29–31. Also available at <https://wwnorton.com/college/history/archive/resources/documents/ch32_04.htm>

"Daddy": Sylvia Plath, *Collected Poems*, Ted Hughes, ed. (Faber & Faber, 1981), 224.

Betty Friedan, *The Feminine Mystique* (W. W. Norton, 1963).

"and Edith Sitwell": For more about Edith Sitwell's influence on Plath, see Marsha Bryant, "Queen Bees: Edith Sitwell, Sylvia Plath & Cross-Atlantic Affiliations," *Feminist Modernist Studies* 2.2 (2019), 194–211.

"'Laurentian,' not 'women's lib'": Ted Hughes to Aurelia Plath, January 12, 1975, MSS 644, Rose Library, Emory University, Atlanta, GA.

"career woman": Sylvia Plath, *The Letters of Sylvia Plath, Vol. 1*, Peter K. Steinberg and Karen V. Kukil, eds. (HarperCollins, 2018), 1084.

"as years spent sleepwalking": See Hilary Holladay, *The Power of Adrienne Rich* (W. W. Norton, 2020).

"the first great poet of childbirth": Anne Stevenson, *Bitter Fame: A Life of Sylvia Plath* (Penguin, 1989; 1998), 234.

"Many of her earliest poems": To date, most of Plath's pre-1956 poems remain unpublished and are housed in her archives at the Lilly Library, Indiana University, and Smith College Special Collections.

"glass caul": *The Unabridged Journals of Sylvia Plath, 1950-1962*, Karen V. Kukil, ed. (Faber & Faber, 2000), 470.

"influenced by the Beats … 'their ponderous armor'": Adam Kirsch, *The Wounded Surgeon: Confession and Transformation in Six American Poets* (W. W. Norton, 2005), 18.

Plath's journal entry on George Abbe: *Journals of Sylvia Plath*, 355.

"'taboo' aesthetic": See Sylvia Plath, interview with Peter Orr, *The Poet Speaks: Interviews with Contemporary Poets* (Barnes & Noble, 1966).

"have distracted … route back in": Elizabeth Gregory, "Confessing the body: gendered poetics" in Jo Gill, ed., *Modern Confessional Writing: New Critical Essays* (Routledge, 2005), 33–49, 41.

"No writer … male literary tradition": Jacqueline Rose, *The Haunting of Sylvia Plath* (Virago, 1991), 28.

"weirdnesses": *Journals of Sylvia Plath*, 520-1.

"walk naked": Yeats ends his poem, "A Coat," with the lines "For there's more enterprise | In walking naked." W. B. Yeats, *Collected Poems*, Richard Finneran, ed. (Macmillan, 1989), 127.

"'extremist' verse": See A. Alvarez, "Beyond the Gentility Principle" in *The New Poetry* (Penguin, 1962).

"functions less as a mirror": Jo Gill, *Anne Sexton's Confessional Poetics* (University Press of Florida, 2007), 51.

"who coined the term 'confessional poetry'": M. L. Rosenthal, "Poetry as Confession," *The Nation* (September 19, 1959).

Rosenthal's excerpt: Interview with Harriet Rosenstein, MSS 1489, Rose Library, Emory University, Atlanta, GA.

"Personal experience is very important": *The Poet Speaks: Interviews with Contemporary Poets*, 169-70.

"My bookcases are overflowing": *Letters of Sylvia Plath, Vol. 1*, 727.

"Women writers whose lives": Hermione Lee, *Biography: A Very Short Introduction* (Oxford University Press, 2009), 128-9.

"a cult": See Janet Badia, *Sylvia Plath and the Mythology of Women Readers* (University of Massachusetts Press, 2011).

"a jet of flame from a literary dragon": "The Blood Jet Is Poetry," *Time* (June 10, 1966), 118–20, 118.

"snake lady of misery": Webster Schott, "The Cult of Plath," *Washington Post Book World* (October 1, 1972), 3.

"as necessary as breathing": see *The Poet Speaks: Interviews with Contemporary Poets.*

"madwoman-as-feminist-rebellion metaphor": Elizabeth J. Donaldson, "The Corpus of the Madwoman: Toward a Feminist Disability Studies Theory of Embodiment and Mental Illness," *NWSA Journal*, 14.3 Feminist Disability Studies (Autumn 2002), 99–119, 102.

"seminal work of feminist criticism": See Sandra Gilbert and Susan Gubar, *The Madwoman in the Attic: The Woman Writer and the Nineteenth-Century Literary Imagination* (Yale University Press, 1979; 2000).

"He was not crazy all the time": Christopher Lehmann-Haupt, "Elizabeth Hardwick, Writer, Dies at 91," *New York Times* (December 4, 2007), A29.

"schizophrenic": Edward Butscher, *Sylvia Plath: Method and Madness* (Seabury Press, 1976), 35.

"a mental hospital, lobotomies": *Letters of Sylvia Plath, Vol. 2*, 967.

"did not have an explicitly political imagination": Sandra Gilbert and Susan Gubar, *No Man's Land: The Place of the Woman Writer in the Twentieth Century, Vol. 3* (Yale University Press, 1994), 297.

"nothing of the social revolutionary in her": Elizabeth Hardwick, "On Sylvia Plath," *New York Review of Books* (August 12, 1971), 3–5.

"exhibits only the most remote": Joyce Carol Oates, "The Death Throes of Romanticism: The Poetry of Sylvia Plath," *Southern Review* 9 (July 1973), 501–22.

Robin Peel, *Writing Back: Sylvia Plath and Cold War Politics* (Fairleigh Dickinson University Press, 2002).

"in high school she co-authored an article": Sylvia Plath and Perry Norton, "Youth's Plea for World Peace," *Christian Science Monitor* (March 16, 1950).

"dissidence": Elaine Showalter, *The Female Malady: Women, Madness and English Culture 1830–1980* (Virago, 1987), 218.

"the philosopher Eric Fromm": Erich Fromm, *The Sane Society* (Holt, Rinehart, and Winston, 1955; 1990).

"as well as R. D. Laing's anti-psychiatry book": R. D. Laing, *The Divided Self: An Existential Study in Sanity and Madness* (Pantheon, 1960; Penguin, 1965).

Memories of Plath's liberal politics come from author interviews with Elizabeth Sigmund (2016) and Perry Norton (2012).

"Recent evidence suggests": Harriet Rosenstein interview with Aurelia Plath, MSS 1489, Rose Library, Emory University, Atlanta, GA.

"Alvarez encouraged": See A. Alvarez, "Beyond the Gentility Principle," *The New Poetry* (Penguin, 1962).

"As Linda Wagner-Martin has written": Linda Wagner-Martin, *The Bell Jar: A Novel of the Fifties* (Twayne Publishers, 1992), 6.

Chapter 2: Origins and ambitions

"gooseflesh . . . being happy": Sylvia Plath, "Ocean 1212-W," in *Johnny Panic and the Bible of Dreams* (Faber & Faber, 1977; 1979), 118.

"I sometimes think": Sylvia Plath, "Ocean 1212-W," in *Johnny Panic*, 117.

"1940s scrapbook": held at Plath MSS II, Lilly Library, Indiana University, Bloomington, IN.

"Snow": Sylvia Plath, "Autograph transcript of 40 juvenile poems." 127550, Literary and Historical Manuscripts, Morgan Library, New York, NY.

"fine, white flying myth": Sylvia Plath, "Ocean 1212-W," in *Johnny Panic*, 124.

"Superman and Paula Brown's New Snowsuit" and "The Shadow" are both collected in Sylvia Plath, *Johnny Panic*.

"A Winter Sunset": *Letters of Sylvia Plath, Vol. 1*, 42–3.

"Fireside Reveries": diary of Sylvia Plath, January 24, 1947, Plath MSS II, Lilly Library, Indiana University, Bloomington, IN.

"her career": Aurelia Plath, "Biographical jottings about Sylvia Plath," Special Collections, Smith College, Northampton, MA.

"several of her other high school short stories": See Heather Clark, *Red Comet: The Short Life and Blazing Art of Sylvia Plath* (Alfred A. Knopf, 2020) for more information about Plath's unpublished high school short stories and poems.

"And Summer Will Not Come Again": *Seventeen* (August 1950), 191; 275–6.

"Portrait": Plath MSS II, Lilly Library, Indiana University, Bloomington, IN.

"Her mother had to scrape": author interview with Betsy Powley Wallingford, 2013.

"ill" and a "sin": *Letters of Sylvia Plath, Vol. 1*, 168.

"Seek No More the Young" and "Youth's Appeal for Peace" are
    both held at Plath MSS II, Lilly Library, Indiana University,
    Bloomington, IN.

"basic brotherhood of all human beings": Sylvia Plath and Perry
    Norton, "Youth's Plea for World Peace," *Christian Science Monitor*
    (March 16, 1950).

"I Am an American": Plath MSS II, Lilly Library, Indiana University,
    Bloomington, IN. An excerpt of this poem is published in *Letters of
    Sylvia Plath, Vol. 1*, 346.

"You're sharp as a pen point": quoted in Margaret Shook, "Sylvia Plath:
    The Poet and the College," *Smith College Alumnae Quarterly* 63.3
    (April 1972), 4–9; 7.

"Sunday at the Mintons": in Sylvia Plath, *Johnny Panic*.

"Mary Ventura": all quotes from this story come from Sylvia Plath,
    Mary Ventura and the Ninth Kingdom (Faber & Faber, 2019).

"abstract paintings": Olive Higgins Prouty to Aurelia Plath,
    December 28, 1955, Plath MSS II, Lilly Library, Indiana University,
    Bloomington, IN.

"desperately Audenesque": see *The Poet Speaks: Interviews with
    Contemporary Poets*.

"Professional Acceptance": *Letters of Sylvia Plath, Vol. 1*, 601.

"the only decent villanelle": Helen Hennessy Vendler to Aurelia Plath,
    September 11, 1954, Plath MSS II, Lilly Library, Indiana University,
    Bloomington, IN.

"Morning in the Hospital Solarium," "Epitaph in Three Parts,"
    and "Lament" can be found in Plath's *Collected Poems*.

Chapter 3: Cold War maladies

"Nancy Hunter, was alarmed": See Nancy Hunter Steiner, *A Closer
    Look at Ariel: A Memory of Sylvia Plath* (Harper's Magazine
    Press, 1973).

"her honors thesis": Sylvia Plath, "The Magic Mirror: A Study of
    the Double in Two of Dostoevsky's Novels" is unpublished and
    held at the Mortimer Rare Book Room, Smith College,
    Northampton, MA.

"she would drag out": "Tongues of Stone," *Johnny Panic*, 268; 270.

"everlasting rising": "Tongues of Stone," *Johnny Panic*, 274.

"beautifully written ... I've ever done": *Letters of Sylvia Plath, Vol. 1*, 880.

"It was a queer, sultry summer": Sylvia Plath, *The Bell Jar* (Heinemann,
    1963; HarperPerennial, 2006), 1.

"There is no yelling" (Plath's ellipsis): *Journals of Sylvia Plath*, 541–2.

"I'm so glad": *The Bell Jar*, 99.

"I wondered what terrible thing": *The Bell Jar*, 143.

"559,000 psychiatric inpatients": Gerald N. Grob, *The Mad Among Us: A History of the Care of America's Mentally Ill* (Free Press, 1994; 2011), 291.

"I had a vision . . . Poison": *The Bell Jar*, 48.

"a whole society can be sick . . . culture itself": Erich Fromm, *The Sane Society* (1955; Holt, 1990), 19; 18; 6.

"Fashion blurbs": *The Bell Jar*, 99.

"artificial and banal": Steiner, *A Closer Look at Ariel*, 44.

"death-in-life": See Amanda Golden, *Annotating Modernism: Marginalia and Pedagogy from Virginia Woolf to the Confessional Poets* (Routledge, 2020).

"Ted Hughes wrote": From Ted Hughes, "Trial" sequence, Add. MS 88993, British Library, London.

Chapter 4: Rebirth and resurrection

"In 1956 she would publish": Sylvia Plath, "Cambridge Letter," *Isis* (May 16, 1956), 9.

"Three Caryatids Without a Portico": Sylvia Plath, *Chequer* 9 (Winter 1956), 3.

"Of the quaint . . . beautiful she may be": Daniel Huws, *Broadsheet* 4 (February 1, 1956), 1–3.

"The Movement": See Blake Morrison, *The Movement: English Poetry and Fiction of the 1950s* (Oxford University Press, 1980).

"the chief holy book of my poetic conscience": *The Letters of Ted Hughes*, Christopher Reid, ed. (Faber & Faber, 2007), 273.

"tight and packed . . . magnificent . . . ingnore [*sic*] me": *Journals of Sylvia Plath*, 207–8.

"Then the worst happened . . . fighting, to you": *Journals of Sylvia Plath*, 211–12.

"Mad passionate abandon": Sylvia Plath, February 25, 1956, 1955–6 calendar, Plath MSS II, Lilly Library, Indiana University, Bloomington, IN.

"dark forces of lust": *Journals of Sylvia Plath*, 214.

"Linda Wagner-Martin . . . the 1950s": *The Bell Jar: A Novel of the Fifties*, 95.

"Pursuit": Sylvia Plath, *Collected Poems*, 22.

"hypnotized . . . making a shift": *Letters of Sylvia Plath, Vol. 1*, 133–4.

"The Wishing Box": *Johnny Panic*, 48–55.

"plagiarizing . . . poor thing . . . my selves now": *Letters of Sylvia Plath, Vol. 1*, 1292–4.

"cheap, flat . . . not even that good": *Letters of Sylvia Plath, Vol. 2*, 94.

"We feel . . . (both misunderstood by many blind people)": *Letters of Sylvia Plath, Vol. 2*, 92.

"We want logic . . . will be changed": *Letters of Sylvia Plath, Vol. 2*, 94.

"so happy his book is accepted first": *Letters of Sylvia Plath, Vol. 2*, 72.

"the very bottom of the pecking order": George Gibian to Harriet Rosenstein, October 18, 1971, MSS 1489, Rose Library, Emory University, Atlanta, GA.

"the art of primitives . . . of inspiration": *Letters of Sylvia Plath, Vol. 2*, 222.

"rococo crystal cage . . . thunderous": *Journals of Sylvia Plath*, 356.

"three terrible . . . clear light": Sylvia Plath, introduction to "The Disquieting Muses" on *The Living Poet*, BBC program recorded October 26, 1960; broadcast November 20, 1960. Sylvia Plath, *The Spoken Word*, audio CD (British Library, 2010).

"The Disquieting Muses": Sylvia Plath, *Collected Poems*, 74–6.

"Mussel Hunter at Rock Harbor": Sylvia Plath, *Collected Poems*, 95–7.

"Lorelei": Sylvia Plath, *Collected Poems*, 94–5.

"Full Fathom Five": Sylvia Plath, *Collected Poems*, 92–3.

"relates more richly . . . dull routine": *Journals of Sylvia Plath*, 381.

"The crown of wire . . . not his own": *Johnny Panic*, 33.

"queer and quite slangy": *Journals of Sylvia Plath*, 441.

"Plath had likely . . . John Holmes": John Holmes Papers, Tufts Archival Research Center, Tufts University, Medford, MA.

"intense breakthrough . . . quite new, quite exciting": *The Poet Speaks: Interviews with Contemporary Poets*, 168.

"I am leaving . . . if anything, 'ugly'": *Letters of Sylvia Plath, Vol. 2*, 305.

"Electra on Azalea Path": Sylvia Plath, *Collected Poems*, 116–17.

"felt so . . . 7 hours a day": *Letters of Sylvia Plath, Vol. 2*, 356.

"the old fall disease": *Journals of Sylvia Plath*, 506.

"Very depressed . . . far from me": *Journals of Sylvia Plath*, 517.

"Helen Vendler": See *Coming of Age as a Poet: Milton, Keats, Eliot, Plath* (Harvard University Press, 2003).

"The Colossus": Sylvia Plath, *Collected Poems*, 129–30.

"a series of madhouse poems": *Journals of Sylvia Plath*, 521.

"Poem for a Birthday": Sylvia Plath, *Collected Poems*, 131–7.

"'real' poetic voice": Ted Hughes, *Winter Pollen: Occasional Prose*, William Scammell, ed. (Picador, 1995), 184.

"weirdnesses": *Journals of Sylvia Plath*, 520–1.

"drawingroom...There I have": *Journals of Sylvia Plath*, 530.

"The Hanging Man": Sylvia Plath, *Collected Poems*, 141–2.

"to make you *hear*...she presents": Richard Howard, review of *The Colossus*, *Poetry* (March 1963), 69–70.

"She steers clear...distinction": A. Alvarez, "Books of the Year," *Observer* (December 18, 1960), 22.

"Zoo Keeper's Wife": Sylvia Plath, *Collected Poems*, 154–5.

"Parliament Hill Fields": Sylvia Plath, *Collected Poems*, 152–3.

"Morning Song": Sylvia Plath, *Collected Poems*, 156–7.

"Tulips": Sylvia Plath, *Collected Poems*, 160–2.

"after major surgery...full return to living": Aurelia Plath to Olive Higgins Prouty, April 18, 1962. Lilly Library, Indiana University, IN.

"In Plaster": Sylvia Plath, *Collected Poems*, 158–60.

"There you are": Ted Hughes, "Trial" sequence, Section 23, Add. MS 88993, British Library.

"the dykes": *Letters of Sylvia Plath, Vol. 2*, 615.

"a terrible block...about anything": *Letters of Sylvia Plath, Vol. 2*, 614–15.

Chapter 5: "The blood jet is poetry"—Devon, London, and *Ariel*

"a happy Heathcliffe": *Letters of Sylvia Plath, Vol. 1*, 1243.

"Wuthering Heights": Sylvia Plath, *Collected Poems*, 167–8.

"exile": *Letters of Sylvia Plath, Vol. 2*, 668.

"'college-educated' mothers": *Letters of Sylvia Plath, Vol. 2*, 693–4.

"exercise devised by Hughes": Sylvia Plath, *Collected Poems*, 291.

"The Moon and the Yew Tree": Sylvia Plath, *Collected Poems*, 172–3.

"How I would...of belief": Sylvia Plath, *Johnny Panic*, 110–11.

"artists and outlanders": *Letters of Sylvia Plath, Vol. 2*, 709.

"upwind": *Letters of Ted Hughes*, 519.

"Context": Sylvia Plath, *Johnny Panic*, 92–3.

"Three Women": Sylvia Plath, *Collected Poems*, 176–87.

"the first great poem of childbirth in the language": Stevenson, *Bitter Fame*, 234.

"Elm": Sylvia Plath, *Collected Poems*, 192–3.

"Event": Sylvia Plath, *Collected Poems*, 194–5.

"The Rabbit Catcher": Sylvia Plath, *Collected Poems*, 193–4.

"the eyes of health": Aurelia Plath, excerpt from unpublished travel
diary, shared by Richard Larschan with author.

"kicks and kids": Nathaniel Tarn, March 12, 1963, diary notes. M1132,
Special Collections and University Archives, Stanford University.

"bitter, frost-bitten, burnt out, averse": Marianne Moore to Judith
Jones, April 7, 1962. Alfred A. Knopf Papers, Harry Ransom Center,
Austin, TX.

"Burning the Letters": Sylvia Plath, *Collected Poems*, 204–5.

"a lost Eden": Sylvia Plath to Elizabeth Compton, February 4, 1963,
MSS 1489, Rose Library, Emory University, GA.

"I was absolutely stunned . . . one comes upon": *Letters of Sylvia Plath,
Vol. 2*, 812. For more about Plath and Sexton, see David Trinidad's
" 'Two Sweet Ladies': Sexton's and Plath's Friendship and Mutual
Influence," *American Poetry Review* 35.6 (2006), 21–9.

"I kept telling myself . . . sweeter companion": *Letters of Sylvia Plath,
Vol. 2*, 880–2.

"All I want . . . without check": *Letters of Sylvia Plath, Vol. 2*, 901.

"The Tour": Sylvia Plath, *Collected Poems*, 237–8.

"The Courage of Shutting Up": Sylvia Plath, *Collected Poems*, 209–10.

"the injunction . . . especially for women": Maggie Nelson, *The Art of
Cruelty: A Reckoning* (W. W. Norton, 2011), 246.

"Stings": Sylvia Plath, *Collected Poems*, 214–15.

"Wintering": Sylvia Plath, *Collected Poems*, 217–19.

"The Applicant": Sylvia Plath, *Collected Poems*, 221–2.

"Daddy": Sylvia Plath, *Collected Poems*, 222–4.

"Her case is complicated . . . free of it": Sylvia Plath, "New Poems"
(BBC introductions), Special Collections, Smith College,
Northampton, MA.

"the bankruptcy of language itself": See Clark's discussion of "Daddy" in
The Grief of Influence: Sylvia Plath and Ted Hughes (Oxford
University Press, 2011).

"Helen Vendler, Irving Howe, Harold Bloom, and Seamus
Heaney": See Helen Vendler, "An Intractable Metal," *New Yorker*
(February 15, 1992), 124; Irving Howe, "A Partial Dissent" in Harold
Bloom, ed., *Sylvia Plath* (Chelsea House, 1989), 5–15; Seamus
Heaney, "The Indefatigable Hoof-taps: Sylvia Plath," *The
Government of the Tongue* (Faber & Faber, 1988), 148–70.

"The Jailer": Sylvia Plath, *Collected Poems*, 226–7.

"Lesbos": Sylvia Plath, *Collected Poems*, 227–30.

"Fever 103°": Sylvia Plath, *Collected Poems*, 231–2.

"Lady Lazarus": Sylvia Plath, *Collected Poems*, 244–7.

"Susan Sontag, who famously questioned": See Susan Sontag, *Regarding the Pain of Others* (Picador, 2004).

"Purdah": Sylvia Plath, *Collected Poems*, 242–4.

"Ariel": Sylvia Plath, *Collected Poems*, 239–40.

"shoots off from": *The Bell Jar*, 72.

"Nick and the Candlestick": Sylvia Plath, *Collected Poems*, 240–2.

"Paul Giles has noted": See Paul Giles, *Virtual Americas: Transnational Fictions and the Transatlantic Imaginary* (Duke University Press, 2004). See also Robin Peel, *Writing Back: Sylvia Plath and Cold War Politics* (Fairleigh Dickinson Press, 2002).

"Standing in a room . . . is aesthetics": Eavan Boland, *A Journey with Two Maps: Becoming a Woman Poet* (Norton, 2011), 158.

"my work should be blessed": *Letters of Sylvia Plath, Vol. 2*, 898.

"Snow Blitz": *Johnny Panic*, 125–33. For more about the British winter of 1962–3, see Juliet Nicolson, *Frostquake: The Frozen Winter of 1962 and how Britain Emerged a Different Country* (Chatto & Windus, 2021).

"according to Hughes": Hughes wrote in an unpublished poem (part of the "Trial" series held in Add. MS 88993 at the British Library) that Plath had wished for stronger reviews of *The Bell Jar* when he visited her in January 1963 to celebrate the book's publication. Plath wrote to others, however, that she was pleased with the book's reviews.

"Plath's . . . review of Donald Hall's": "New Comment—a review of 'Contemporary American Poetry'" is on the audio CD *The Spoken Word: Sylvia Plath* (British Library, 2010).

"Sheep in Fog": Sylvia Plath, *Collected Poems*, 262.

"Kindness": Sylvia Plath, *Collected Poems*, 269–70.

"Words": Sylvia Plath, *Collected Poems*, 270.

"Balloons": Sylvia Plath, *Collected Poems*, 271–2.

"Edge": Sylvia Plath, *Collected Poems*, 272–3.

"the long fall from grace": Eavan Boland, *Outside History: Selected Poems 1980-1990* (Norton, 1990; 2001), 139.

"frozen and eternal tableau": Judith Kroll, *Chapters in a Mythology: The Poetry of Sylvia Plath* (Harper & Row, 1976; Sutton, 2007), 153.

"protective": Helen Vendler, *Coming of Age as a Poet: Milton, Keats, Eliot, Plath* (Harvard University Press, 2003), 146.

"What appals me . . . the edge of madness": *Letters of Sylvia Plath, Vol. 2*, 967–9.

Chapter 6: Afterlives

"tragic death...modern poets, Ted Hughes": Anon., "Tragic Death of Young Authoress," *St Pancras Chronicle* (February 22, 1963), AA 33.

"died suddenly...inestimable": A. Alvarez, "A Poet's Epitaph," *Observer*, February 17, 1963.

"Have you read...never come about": Thomas Travisano and Saskia Hamilton, eds., *Words in Air: The Complete Correspondence Between Elizabeth Bishop and Robert Lowell* (Farrar, Straus and Giroux, 2008), 513.

"infuriated feminist critics": See Marjorie Perloff, "The Two Ariels: The (Re)Making of the Sylvia Plath Canon," in Neil Fraistat, ed., *Poems in Their Place: The Intertextuality and Order of Poetic Collections* (University of North Carolina Press, 1986), 308–33.

"Patron Saint": Keith Sagar, *Poet and Critic: The Letters of Ted Hughes & Keith Sagar*, Keith Sagar, ed. (British Library, 2012), 108.

"'Laurentian,' not 'women's lib'": Ted Hughes to Aurelia Plath, January 12, 1975, MSS 644, Rose Library, Emory University, GA.

"enemy country": *Poet and Critic: The Letters of Ted Hughes & Keith Sagar*, 282.

"Her Kind": Anne Sexton, *To Bedlam and Part Way Back* (Houghton Mifflin, 1960), 21.

"a priestess...cult": A. Alvarez, *The Savage God: A Study of Suicide* (Weidenfeld & Nicolson, 1971; W. W. Norton, 1990), 46.

"I am a damn good high priestess": *Letters of Sylvia Plath, Vol. 1*, 781.

"By 1993, when Janet Malcolm published..." See Janet Malcolm, *The Silent Woman: Sylvia Plath and Ted Hughes* (Vintage, 1995).

"Sylvia's relationships...fear of abandonment": Linda Wagner-Martin, *Sylvia Plath: A Biography* (Simon & Schuster, 1987), 41.

"Sylvia...was indeed cursed": Stevenson, *Bitter Fame*, 32–3.

"Haunted...threatened her frail being": Stevenson, *Bitter Fame*, 3.

"addicted...interior hollowness": Andrew Wilson, *Mad Girl's Love Song: Sylvia Plath and Life Before Ted* (Scribner, 2013), 39; 89.

"Writing about women...the pillory, or the head in the oven": Caroline Fraser, "On Robert Caro, Great Men, and the Problem of Powerful Women in Biography," *Lit Hub* (May 16, 2019). <https://lithub.com/on-robert-caro-great-men-and-the-problem-of-powerful-women-in-biography/>

"I wondered what": *The Bell Jar*, 143.

"Power and ambition in women": Fraser, "On Robert Caro..."

"In 2020, I published": see Heather Clark, *Red Comet: The Short Life and Blazing Art of Sylvia Plath* (Knopf, 2020).

"one of the very few ... modern poetry": George Steiner, *Language and Silence: Essays on Language, Literature, and the Inhuman* (Yale University Press, 1970; 1998), 301.

"monstrous": Irving Howe, "A Partial Dissent," in Harold Bloom, ed., *Sylvia Plath* (Chelsea House, 1989), 5–15, 12.

"gratuitous and humanly offensive": *Sylvia Plath*, 3.

"so tangled up": Seamus Heaney, "The Indefatigable Hoof-taps: Sylvia Plath," *The Government of the Tongue* (Faber & Faber, 1988), 148–70, 165.

"tantrum": Helen Vendler, "An Intractable Metal," *New Yorker* (February 15, 1992), 124.

"prompted the critic": see Jacqueline Rose, *The Haunting of Sylvia Plath* (Virago, 1991).

"birdies still go tweet-tweet": *Letters of Sylvia Plath, Vol. 2*, 874–5.

"When the curtain goes down": Elizabeth Hardwick, quoted in Stevenson, *Bitter Fame*, 298.

"dehumanize people": Joyce Carol Oates, "The Death Throes of Romanticism: The Poetry of Sylvia Plath," *Southern Review* 9 (July 1973), 501–22.

"Janet Badia, Judith Kroll, Susan Gubar and Sandra Gilbert, Tracy Brain, Steven Gould Axelrod, Robin Peel, Jacqueline Rose, Christina Britzolakis, Tim Kendall, Susan Van Dyne, Lynda Bundtzen, Gail Crowther and Peter K. Steinberg": For Badia, Kroll, Gubar and Gilbert, Peel, Brain, and Rose: see previous citations. See "Additional further reading" below for citations of other works.

"his poetic sequence about Plath": see Ted Hughes, *Birthday Letters* (Faber & Faber, 1998).

Additional further reading

Axelrod, Steven Gould. *Sylvia Plath: The Wound and the Cure of Words*. Johns Hopkins Press, 1990.

Bayley, Sally and Tracy Brain, eds. *Representing Sylvia Plath*. Cambridge University Press, 2011.

Brain, Tracy, ed. *Sylvia Plath in Context*. Cambridge University Press, 2019.

Bundtzen, Lynda. *The Other Ariel*. University of Massachusetts Press, 2001.

Butscher, Edward, ed. *Sylvia Plath: The Woman and the Work*. Dodd, Mead & Co., 1977.

Clark, Heather. *The Grief of Influence: Sylvia Plath and Ted Hughes*. Oxford University Press, 2011.

Connors, Kathleen and Sally Bayley, eds. *Eye Rhymes: Sylvia Plath's Art of the Visual*. Oxford University Press, 2007.

Crowther, Gail and Peter K. Steinberg, *These Ghostly Archives: The Unearthing of Sylvia Plath*. Fonthill Media, 2017.

Davison, Peter. *The Fading Smile: Poets in Boston from Robert Frost to Robert Lowell to Sylvia Plath*. W. W. Norton, 1996.

Ferreter, Luke. *Sylvia Plath's Fiction: A Critical Study*. Edinburgh University Press, 2012.

Gill, Jo, ed., *The Cambridge Companion to Sylvia Plath*. Cambridge University Press, 2006.

Golden, Amanda, Anita Helle, and Maeve O'Brien, eds. *The Bloomsbury Handbook to Sylvia Plath*. Bloomsbury, 2021.

Goodspeed-Chadwick, Julie. *Reclaiming Assia Wevill: Sylvia Plath, Ted Hughes, and the Literary Imagination*. Louisiana State University Press, 2019.

Gourley, James. "The same anew: James Joyce's Modernism and its Influence on Sylvia Plath's *Bell Jar*." *College Literature* 45.4 (Fall 2018), 695–723.

Helle, Anita, ed. *The Unraveling Archive: Essay on Sylvia Plath*. University of Michigan Press, 2007.

Kendall, Tim. *Sylvia Plath: A Critical Study*. Faber & Faber, 2001.

Ostriker, Alicia. *Stealing the Language: The Emergence of Women's Poetry in America*. Beacon Press, 1987.

Van Dyne, Susan. *Revising Life: Sylvia Plath's Ariel Poems*. University of North Carolina Press, 1993.

Wooten, Will. *The Alvarez Generation: Thom Gunn, Geoffrey Hill, Ted Hughes, Sylvia Plath, and Peter Porter*. Liverpool University Press, 2015.

Index

For the benefit of digital users, indexed terms that span two pages (e.g., 52–53) may, on occasion, appear on only one of those pages.

DEPRESSION
A Very Short Introduction
Jan Scott and Mary Jane Tacchi

What is depression? What is bipolar disorder? How are they diagnosed and how are they treated?

In this *Very Short Introduction*, Jan Scott and Mary Jane Tacchi give an informative account of the changing understandings of depression, manic depression and bipolar disorder, and the new treatments available to people suffering from depression—from antidepressants to mood stabilizers. They explore the association between mood disorders and physical illness, as well as the link between creativity and depression in modern-day society. Scott and Tacchi also consider what may lie ahead for those living with depression.

LOVE
A Very Short Introduction
Ronald de Sousa

Erotic love has been celebrated in art and poetry as life's most rewarding and exalting experience, worth living and dying for and bringing out the best in ourselves. *And yet it has excused, and even been thought to justify, the most reprehensible crimes. Why should this be?*

This *Very Short Introduction* explores this and other puzzling questions. Ronald de Sousa considers some of the many paradoxes created by love, looking at the different kinds of love (affections, affiliation, *philia*, *storage*, and *agape*) with a focus on *eros*, or romantic love. He considers whether our conventional beliefs about love and sex are deeply irrational and argues that alternative conceptions of love and sex, although hard to formulate and live by, may be worth striving for.

www.oup.com/vsi

THE MEANING OF LIFE

A Very Short Introduction

Terry Eagleton

'Philosophers have an infuriating habit of analysing questions rather than answering them', writes Terry Eagleton, who, in these pages, asks the most important question any of us ever ask, and attempts to answer it. So what is the meaning of life? In this witty, spirited, and stimulating inquiry, Eagleton shows how centuries of thinkers - from Shakespeare and Schopenhauer to Marx, Sartre and Beckett - have tackled the question. Refusing to settle for the bland and boring, Eagleton reveals with a mixture of humour and intellectual rigour how the question has become particularly problematic in modern times. Instead of addressing it head-on, we take refuge from the feelings of 'meaninglessness' in our lives by filling them with a multitude of different things: from football and sex, to New Age religions and fundamentalism.

'Light hearted but never flippant.'

The Guardian.